Interaction Online

Cambridge Handbooks for Language Teachers

This series, now with over 50 titles, offers practical ideas, techniques and activities for the teaching of English and other languages, providing inspiration for both teachers and trainers.

Recent titles in this series:

Teach Business English
SYLVIE DONNA

Teaching English Spelling
A practical guide
RUTH SHEMESH and SHEILA WALLER

Using Folktales
ERIC K. TAYLOR

Learner English (Second edition)
A teacher's guide to interference and other problems
EDITED BY MICHAEL SWAN and BERNARD SMITH

Planning Lessons and Courses
Designing sequences of work for the language classroom
TESSA WOODWARD

Teaching Large Multilevel Classes
NATALIE HESS

Using the Board in the Language Classroom
JEANNINE DOBBS

Writing Simple Poems
Pattern poetry for language acquisition
VICKI L. HOLMES and MARGARET R. MOULTON

Laughing Matters
Humour in the language classroom
PÉTER MEDGYES

Stories
Narrative activities in the language classroom
RUTH WAJNRYB

Using Authentic Video in the Language Classroom
JANE SHERMAN

Extensive Reading Activities for Teaching Language
EDITED BY JULIAN BAMFORD and RICHARD R. DAY

Language Activities for Teenagers
EDITED BY SETH LINDSTROMBERG

Pronunciation Practice Activities
A resource book for teaching English pronunciation
MARTIN HEWINGS

Drama Techniques (Third edition)
A resource book of communication activities for language teachers
ALAN MALEY and ALAN DUFF

Five-Minute Activities for Business English
PAUL EMMERSON and NICK HAMILTON

Games for Language Learning (Third edition)
ANDREW WRIGHT, DAVID BETTERIDGE and MICHAEL BUCKBY

Dictionary Activities
CINDY LEANEY

Dialogue Activities
Exploring spoken interaction in the language class
NICK BILBROUGH

Five-Minute Activities for Young Learners
PENNY MCKAY and JENNI GUSE

The Internet and the Language Classroom (Second edition)
A practical guide for teachers
GAVIN DUDENEY

Working with Images
A resource book for the language classroom
BEN GOLDSTEIN

Grammar Practice Activities (Second edition)
A practical guide for teachers
PENNY UR

Intercultural Language Activities
JOHN CORBETT

Learning One-to-One
INGRID WISNIEWSKA

Communicative Activities for EAP
JENNI GUSE

Memory Activities for Language Learning
NICK BILBROUGH

Vocabulary Activities
PENNY UR

Classroom Management Techniques
JIM SCRIVENER

CLIL Activities
A resource for subject and language teachers
LIZ DALE and ROSIE TANNER

Language Learning with Technology
Ideas for integrating technology in the classroom
GRAHAM STANLEY

Translation and Own-language Activities
PHILIP KERR

Language Learning with Digital Video
BEN GOLDSTEIN and PAUL DRIVER

Discussions and More
Oral fluency practice in the classroom
PENNY UR

Interaction Online

Lindsay Clandfield and Jill Hadfield

Consultant and editor: Scott Thornbury

CAMBRIDGE
UNIVERSITY PRESS

CAMBRIDGE
UNIVERSITY PRESS

University Printing House, Cambridge CB2 8BS, United Kingdom

One Liberty Plaza, 20th Floor, New York, NY 10006, USA

477 Williamstown Road, Port Melbourne, VIC 3207, Australia

314-321, 3rd Floor, Plot 3, Splendor Forum, Jasola District Centre, New Delhi-110025, India

79 Anson Road, #06-04/06, Singapore 079906

Cambridge University Press is part of the University of Cambridge.

It furthers the University's mission by disseminating knowledge in the pursuit of education, learning and research at the highest international levels of excellence.

www.cambridge.org
Information on this title: www.cambridge.org/9781316629178

© Cambridge University Press 2017

First published 2017

20 19 18 17 16 15 14 13 12 11 10 9 8 7 6 5 4 3 2 1

A catalogue record for this publication is available from the British Library

ISBN 978-1-316-62917-8 Paperback
ISBN 978-1-316-62921-5 Apple ibook
ISBN 978-1-316-62920-8 Google ebook
ISBN 978-1-316-62919-2 Kindle ebook
ISBN 978-1-316-62922-2 ebooks.com ebook

Additional resources for this publication at http://esource.cambridge.org/interactiononline

Cambridge University Press has no responsibility for the persistence or accuracy of URLs for external or third-party internet websites referred to in this publication, and does not guarantee that any content on such websites is, or will remain, accurate or appropriate.

Contents

Thanks

This book would not have been possible without the support of Scott Thornbury, Karen Momber, and especially Jo Timerick. Our thanks to them, and to our very thorough and professional editor Helen Forrest.

We'd also like to thank the students and teachers who helped in the trialling of this book. This includes teachers and students at the Universidad Peruana de Ciencias Aplicadas (thank you to Iriana Milagros for organizing this!), fellow teachers on the Consultants-E E-moderation courses, the students who gave their time to participate on our Project Interact, ELT Writers Connected for their feedback on Collaborative Stories Melody Mason and Angela Desmarais and their lovely students in Module 3 Academic English and Class 3 GE for their enthusiastic participation, creative responses and valuable feedback.

Lindsay would like to thank Nicky Hockly and Gavin Dudeney of The Consultants-E, who trained him originally as an online tutor and have given him lots of opportunities in the field of E-moderation. He'd also like to give special mention to BG, ckyrias, cooldeals, dazza, Epi, joshzam, Pershy, Ragian, Winston and other online friends who have never been shy to try out new and crazy forum games.

Jill would like to thank Laura and Charlie for their support and encouragement through the writing of this book.

Acknowledgements

The authors and publishers acknowledge the following sources of copyright material and are grateful for the permissions granted. While every effort has been made, it has not always been possible to identify the sources of all the material used, or to trace all copyright holders. If any omissions are brought to our notice, we will be happy to include the appropriate acknowledgements on reprinting and in the next update to the digital edition, as applicable.

Text Acknowledgements:

SAGE Publications for the text on p. 2 adapted from 'The Rhetoric of ICT and the New Language of Learning: A Critical Analysis of the Use of ICT in the Curricular Field' by Geir Haugsbakk and Yngve Nordkvelle, *European Educational Research Journal*, 6(1), pp. 1–12, March 2007. Copyright © 2007 European Educational Research Journal. Reproduced with kind permission of SAGE Publications Ltd; Mangodew Publishing for the text on p. 96 adapted from 'Best Way to Enjoy Household Chores: Extreme Ironing in Strange Places' by Keremcan Ayhan, Adventure Herald website, 09.09.2015. Copyright © Mangodew Publishing. Reproduced with kind permission of Mangodew Publishing; Rube Goldberg Inc. for the text on p. 126 adapted from 'Rube Goldberg's Self-Operating Napkin'. Artwork Copyright © and TM Rube Goldberg Inc. All Rights Reserved. RUBE GOLDBERG ® is a registered trademark of Rube Goldberg Inc. All materials used with permission. rubegoldberg.com; Laureate International Universities for the text on pp. 198–199 adapted from 'Rubrics extract for grammar and vocabulary control in an online writing activity'. Copyright © Laureate International Universities. Reproduced with kind permission of Universidad Peruana de Ciencias Aplicadas – UPC, Laureate International Universities; Harriet W. Sheridan Center for Teaching and Learning for the text on pp. 199–200 adapted from 'Peer Assessment in Online Courses'. Copyright © Harriet W. Sheridan Center for Teaching and Learning. Reproduced with kind permission of Harriet W. Sheridan Center for Teaching and Learning, Brown University.

Photo Acknowledgements:

L = Left, R = Right, C = Centre, TL = Top Left, TR = Top Right, TC = Top Centre

p. 6 (Lindsay): © Lindsay Clandfield; p. 7: Ariel Skelley/Blend Images/Getty Images; p. 16: © Jill Hadfield; p. 85: Dea/Boccardi/De Agostini Picture Library/Getty Images; p. 92 (L): Westend61/Getty Images; p. 92 (C): Mint Images - Frans Lanting/Mint Images/Getty Images; p. 92(R): AntonioGuillem/ iStock/Getty Images Plus/Getty Images; p. 96: Mark Greenwood/Moment Mobile/Getty Images ; p. 110: Westend61/Getty Images; p. 111(TL): Gregory Adams/Moment/Getty Images; p. 111 (TC): Sir Francis Canker Photography/Moment/Getty Images; p. 111 (TR): Anthony Brawley Photography/ Moment/Getty Images; p. 112: Andrew Rich/E+/Getty Images; p. 130: Martin Child/Photolibrary/ Getty Images; p. 163: Sebastien Varone/EyeEm/Getty Images; p. 169: © Dublin airport; p. 180: Ferdousi Begum/EyeEm/Getty Images.

Illustration by: p. 125: Rube Goldberg (Self-Operating Napkin).

Introduction

Who is this book for?

This is a resource book for teachers interested in incorporating an aspect of interaction online in their language courses. This introduction addresses the notion and importance of interaction online as a component not only of online courses, but also of blended and face-to-face courses. The book contains more than 75 activities, which all involve online interaction, but are not just for fully-online courses. They can be used in online courses, but also in courses requiring an element of blended learning or part-time courses requiring the teacher to set some out-of-classroom work. This book could also be used on courses that are fully face-to-face, but where the teacher would like to ring the changes on traditional written homework.

Interaction Online will be useful to teachers in secondary, tertiary and adult sectors, both in private language institutions and in the state sector. The activities cover a range of levels with suggestions for adaptation, so they will be useful to a wide range of learners.

The book can be used in institutions that have platforms such as Blackboard or Moodle for learning support through to institutions which have no official platforms; in the latter case all activities may be used on easily available applications such as Facebook, Skype or chat rooms. The book thus has relevance to a wide range of teachers, learning situations and institutional settings.

The changing educational landscape

In many language teaching situations worldwide, students are expected to do a proportion of their language learning work outside the classroom. While this has traditionally taken the form of homework, the situation now has changed considerably, due to five important trends:

- the ubiquity of the internet and mobile devices which can connect to the internet and which therefore afford the learner more chances to access English
- the spread of online learning, through completely online courses, apps or blended options
- the explosion of educational technology platforms and apps which are making it easier and cheaper to set up an online element of a language course
- the pressure on school budgets to increase student numbers without increasing face-to-face contact hours with a teacher, meaning that many courses are being offered with an online component
- an emphasis on lifelong learning and independent learning in education systems around the world, emphasized by the adoption of elements of documents such as the Common European Framework of Reference (CEFR).

Work done outside the physical classroom can vary from courses taught completely online, to blended learning courses, to schools with part-time students who are expected to do around 10 hours work a week outside class hours.

This online work has been heralded by and large as a 'good thing'. Arguments in favour of online or blended courses often emphasize the benefits of students being able to learn when and where they want, and to control the pace of their own learning. Modern learning apps and platforms are getting more and more attractive and increasingly include elements of gamification, rewarding learners with points and badges for work accomplished. Manufacturers of these programmes argue that these features maintain, or increase motivation.

When it comes to all this change, teachers are often caught between the requirements to adapt constantly to the changing online scenario and to create lessons and materials for outside the classroom as well as face-to-face teaching. It is our hope that this book will remove some of that burden for them!

Interactive, interaction, interactivity

It is relatively easy for teachers to point students to listening and reading texts, which abound online. There are also an enormous number of language practice activities for grammar, vocabulary and pronunciation. While these are often of varying quality, publishers are beginning to put more and more professionally edited materials online as part of their course offerings.

Many of these resources claim to be interactive. The history of the term 'interactive' in education technology is an interesting one. Beginning in the 1980s and 1990s, the term gained currency among developers, designers and marketers of educational technology programmes. Almost every technology and approach was labelled 'interactive'. According to the Norwegian scholars Geir Haugsbakk and Yngve Nordkvelle:

> 'Interactivity' was obviously quite useful for marketing the new technology. The term had no commonly accepted meaning or definitions, but a whole range of positive connotations made it acceptable for most people. One of the prominent ideas was interactive technology establishing and supporting quite new ways of learning in contrast to the established ones. Interactive technology should open up student activity, user control and dialogue. The focus was put on learning rather than teaching. The concepts of 'teaching' and 'learning' were introduced as a dichotomy, to a large extent based on quite simple stereotypes of the two phenomena – teaching as something bad we had to get rid of and learning as something good that we have to promote. (Haugsbakk and Nordkvelle, 2007, p. 3)

This suggests that in technology, interactivity takes place between human and machine, rather than human and human. It also suggests that tech marketing promotes the simplistic idea that educational technology equates with learning, which involves interaction (human–machine) and is good, whereas the traditional face-to-face classroom equates with teaching which involves lecture-style transmission (teacher–student) and is bad.

However, Mark Callagher makes a distinction between the computer use of the word and the educational use which contrasts with this simplistic equation, recognizing that teaching, rather than being a one-way transmission model, involves far more complex interactions than are possible in human–machine interaction:

> To interact, as defined by the Oxford Dictionary, is a verb meaning to 'act so as to have a reciprocal effect'. In computer terms interactive refers to a two-way flow of information between the computer

and the user. This second meaning is very basic and to be expected in all spheres of computer use these days anyhow.

In educational theory interactivity has been defined more broadly as 'communication, participation and feedback' (Muirhead, 1999) or as 'an interplay and exchange in which individuals and groups influence each other' (Roblyer and Ekhaml, 2000). (Callagher, 2008, p. 8)

Some researchers have attempted to draw a terminological distinction between interaction (focusing on people's behaviour) and interactivity (focusing on characteristics of technology) (see Wagner 1994, 1997). But, by and large, the word 'interactive' and its derivatives have been mostly appropriated to refer to how people relate to software.

Terminology notwithstanding, educational software from the 1980s and 1990s was interactive in a very weak way. The learner interacted with the program, normally through drag-and-drop exercises, gapfills and multiple choice quizzes. This human–machine interaction was very different from the human–human kind of interaction that was being promoted in communicative language classrooms across the world at the same time. It is this second form of interaction that we are concerned with here. We refer to this human–human interaction as 'strong' interaction, as distinguished from 'weak' interaction (human–machine interaction of the above kind).

The quality of interaction in online language courses

We believe that, while education technology has made considerable advances since the 1990s, the same weak interaction in online courses prevails. While online courses and learning platforms may include tools that can facilitate strong interaction between participants, these are often underused. A discussion forum may end up being simply a virtual bulletin board for the instructor to post announcements. A chat room feature may be empty most of the time. And as the number of students enrolled in a single online class gets bigger and bigger, institutions may be tempted to include more and more 'interactive' quizzes, videos and audio clips, all of which feature automated marking and therefore need little attention from the teacher.

This is not necessarily inherently the fault of technology. If the explosion of social media has taught us one thing, it is that people enjoy strong interaction with each other through the use of technology. In this respect, technology can have a profound effect in assisting human interaction. But in online English language courses, or online elements of blended courses, learners are often forced to 'go it alone'. This in part explains why online courses suffer so often from poor user motivation and high drop-out rates. It may also explain why the online element of blended courses is under-utilized. The recent trend in gamification of educational products, by adding points and badges for getting through the material, can only work for a limited time and for a certain kind of learner. Interacting with others is one of the reasons people enjoy language classes so much.

There is much research in the area of interaction and motivation on online courses which is applicable here. Rebecca Croxton offers a survey of the research on why students may drop out of online courses and finds that lack of interactivity is a prime factor. She argues, 'When students have insufficient formal or informal interaction experiences in online courses, both learning and satisfaction may be compromised.' (Croxton, 2014, p. 315)

Other studies have found that decreased social interactivity can lead to lowered satisfaction among students and increased feelings of isolation, disillusionment, and greater risk of dropping out of the online learning environment (Liu, Magjuka, Bonk and Lee, 2007; Morris, Finnegan and Wu, 2005; Tello, 2007).

All this suggests that human–machine interactivity is not enough to maintain student satisfaction and engagement in online learning. There are also other important pedagogical reasons for incorporating human interaction into online learning.

Reasons for using interaction in online courses

Callagher suggests that student–student interaction is not only motivating and engaging, but actually essential for learning to take place, and sees participation in online discussion as an opportunity for this:

> When students participate in online discussions they are exposed to a broader range of views allowing them to develop more diverse perspectives and to collaborate in the construction of new meaning. (Callagher, 2008, p. 11)

This of course is true of face-to-face interaction in the classroom, but Callagher finds a special benefit of online discussion can be linked to its asynchronous nature:

> The anytime aspect of online discussion allows learners to have time to think deeper about a topic and respond when they feel more informed or inspired. (Bender, 2003)

In addition, Chen and Looi (2007) find that 'online discussion provides a permanent record of one's thoughts for later students' reflection and debate'.

Croxton and Callagher also make points about the benefits of the written nature of online discussion for shyer or more reticent students, who like the opportunity to reflect before they write, and feel less intimidated than in a face-to-face discussion, and less dominated by more vocal students. In this situation, asynchronous online communication (that is not occurring in real time, as opposed to synchronous real time communication) is beneficial:

> Communicating asynchronously via online bulletin boards can offer learners the opportunity to express their thoughts without restraint and students are more willing to ask questions and participate through discussion groups. In an extensive review of literature concerning social learning theory and web-based learning environments, Hill et al. (2009) found that because asynchronous social interaction in web-based learning environments is not as immediate as that found in a physical setting, some learners use this delay in responses to reflect before they write. (Croxton, 2014, p. 316)

> 'Students can feel more comfortable sharing comments in this format which they perceive to be less threatening than an intimidating face-to-face environment.' (Ng and Cheung, 2007; Frazee, 2003) Shy and less vocal students felt strongly that there was more opportunity to share their opinions without being interrupted by dominant students.' (Ng and Cheung, 2007; Bender, 2003). (Callagher, 2008, p. 11)

All of this suggests to us that having online, asynchronous interaction in a language course (fully online, part online or even face-to-face) is extremely beneficial for the learner's self-confidence and motivation.

Principles of interaction

This book is about redressing that balance of weak and strong interaction in online elements of language courses. It is about including more interaction between and among learners and the instructor, rather than between learners and the software. To this end, we think it might be best to outline some principles of what, in our mind, interaction means in an online course. Interaction:

- is between human and human, not human and machine
- can involve voice or text
- can be synchronous or asynchronous
- should have a reason for communication, i.e. to share information, opinions, values or ideas
- should have a purpose and have closure in an end-point: communication should achieve something (the solution to a puzzle for example, or the creation of a text or artefact)
- should involve two-way participation: members should both take account of others' contributions and contribute themselves
- should involve all members of the group
- should involve topics that are interesting and motivating
- should include a range of topics and interaction-types to appeal to different learner preferences.

Tools for online interaction

There are lots of technological tools that facilitate interaction, and new ones are coming out all the time. Other tools disappear and are replaced by new ones. However, we did not want this book to be an explanation or showcase of the latest tools, many of which may have become obsolete by the time you read this.

Instead, we choose to focus on two generic kinds of tool, discussion forums and instant messaging, that have not lost their popularity since they first appeared online over 30 years ago. We also include a third tool, audio/videoconferencing, that has only recently become more accessible and common in online courses.

Discussion forums or message boards

A discussion forum tool allows participants to post a message and read other people's messages. This is usually done asynchronously (i.e. not in real time). Depending on the tool, a discussion forum may allow you to attach images, sounds, video and other files to it.

A good discussion forum will allow for threaded discussions, where the replies to one post are organized underneath it for ease of reading. An example is shown in Figure 0.1. Another useful feature to look out for in discussion forums is a 'quote' button, enabling you to copy and paste something said by another participant automatically and respond to it.

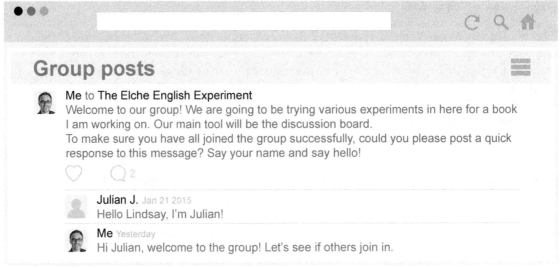

Figure 0.1: Sample discussion forum

Instant message services or chats

An instant message service (e.g. Figure 0.2) or chat service (e.g. Figure 0.3) allows the participants to type messages to each other in real time. Current tools allow participants to attach audio, image and video files to a message. Unlike discussion forums, chats and instant message services are mainly used for synchronous (i.e. real time and simultaneous) communication.

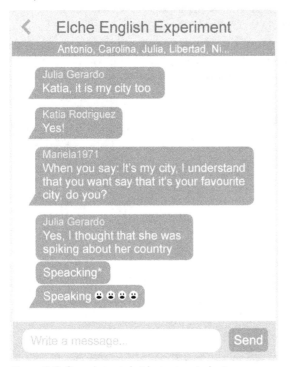

Figure 0.2: Sample text chat between students on an instant message forum

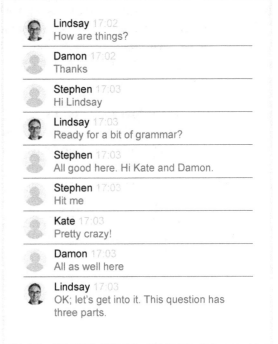

Figure 0.3: Sample text chat room

Audio or videoconferencing

As broadband and high-speed internet increases in spread, real-time audio and videoconferencing are becoming more and more common in online courses. An example is shown in Figure 0.4. The tools for these will vary in features but will allow multiple participants to speak (or speak and see each other) at once and are therefore used mostly for synchronous activity.

At the time of writing, many online language courses have at least two of these tools. Most teachers are familiar with communicating via all of these formats. We have decided to focus most of our activities on the first two tools, as these are the easiest to use and still extremely popular. Audio and videoconferencing, at the time of writing, still often suffer from connection speeds and time lag but are growing in popularity.

Figure 0.4: Videoconferencing

Implications for teaching and learning

One of the most powerful reasons for including more and more automated exercises and interactive software in online elements of courses is that it saves teachers time and effort, thus allowing them to spend more time on creative lesson planning. It can also be economically advantageous. It is very tempting for educational institutions to increase the number of students on such a course. The machine can mark one or one thousand exercises and does not get tired, or charge more per hour.

However, as we have seen, such policies will not help learning in the long run. What is more, an over-reliance on automated interaction may result in higher drop-out levels on online courses.

If you are a teacher or educational leader who wishes to have more effective online elements of your courses then the implications are clear: strong interaction between the participants on your courses is necessary. For this interaction to be successful, however, it takes work on the part of the teacher. It also takes time, and it is more successful with smaller groups. These three facts are well known to English teachers, as they are what has made successful face-to-face language classes for many years!

You also need ideas and examples of activities which promote strong interaction between learners online, and that are suitable for language classes. That is where this book can help. This book also offers you guidance on setting up and managing online interaction, using the student-produced texts for feedback, error correction and assessment, and designing your own online activities.

How this book is organized

Callagher (2008) suggests that most use of online interaction has taken place in the tertiary sector, where in blended or online courses the discussion board or forum takes the place of a seminar. This means that these discussion forums are most extensively used, as their name suggests, for intellectual debate and argument. We wish to extend this use of discussion forums to include different interaction and activity types. We have divided the activities in this book according to different kinds of strong interaction, of which we identify five: personal, factual, creative, critical and fanciful.

Personal interaction

This kind of interaction involves an exchange of personal information. The classic 'find someone who' classroom activity is an example of this. Sharing photos or personal stories, and commenting or reacting to these are further examples familiar to anyone who has been on social media.
Activity types include:
- posting an image of something important to you
- questions and answers on a personal topic (e.g. your family, your town, your job)
- telling a personal story
- sharing your feelings
- informal chit-chat.

Factual interaction

This kind of interaction involves sharing information on a factual topic. Information gap and guessing games are examples of factual interaction.
Activity types include:
- asking questions about a photo of a real person or place
- sharing information about a famous person's biography
- answering questions about a subject you know about
- interviewing an expert on a topic to find more information
- helping to identify a location on a map.

Creative interaction

This involves interaction between the participants in order to create a 'product': a story, poem, advert, etc.

Activity types include:

- collaborative story-writing
- imagining and sharing the 'stories' behind everyday things
- creating a collaborative poem.

Critical interaction

This kind of interaction involves an exchange of opinions on a topic or topics. Discussions, debates or role plays can all be occasions for critical interaction.

Activity types here include:

- debating the pros and cons of a topic
- considering causes and consequences
- ranking items or ideas
- playing devil's advocate
- looking at a topic from a different point of view
- sharing your opinion on a topic.

Fanciful interaction

This type of interaction is often used on online games. It involves entering into an imaginary situation, perhaps (but not necessarily) taking on a role and interacting to solve a puzzle or share information.

Activity types include:

- role playing
- rewriting parts of a story
- brainstorming a solution to a fantasy problem.

These categories will appeal to different learners' preferences for activities they enjoy and find motivating. Four dichotomies are involved:

- **affective vs cognitive:** some activities involve the affective and emotional side, the sharing of values and feelings, while others involve logic and argument.
- **fact vs fantasy:** some interactions involve real-life situations, while some involve fantasy situations.
- **exploratory vs solution-based activities:** this is essentially the distinction between activities that allow learners to use their imagination to create something new and original, and activities that challenge learners to find the right answer.
- **immediate vs reflective activities:** some activities, such as guessing games, are 'quick-fire', requiring an immediate response, while others, such as discussions or story creation, demand a more reflective delayed response time.

All the activities are closed-task, or convergent, that is, they have an end-point: the completion of a task, the solution of a puzzle, the guessing of a conundrum, or the creation of a poem or story. The reason behind this is that that sense of achievement resulting from successful completion of a task is very satisfying and leads to self-esteem and increased motivation. It is also important to have a fixed end-point in an online activity for practical reasons, so that the teacher knows when the activity is finished. This is more difficult to ascertain than in a classroom situation, where the teacher can see when an activity is finished or students have run out of things to say. Some activities make use of a ludic game-format, for example, guessing or puzzle solving; some require the completion of a task, resulting in for example, a group decision; and some require the collaborative creation of a product, for example a group advert or poem.

How the activities are organized

The activities have a standard framework, making it easy for teachers to move from one activity to another:
- A box at the top of each activity which teachers can use to see at a glance whether the activity will be suitable for their class. The box specifies the following:
  o Outline: the kind of activity students will be involved in
  o Level
  o Learning focus: grammar, functions or vocabulary practised
  o Time required for the activity and any post-activity follow-up
  o Preparation: what needs to be done in advance of posting the activity online (not all activities require preparation).
- Procedure: step-by step instructions for how to use the activity.
- Tasks to be posted online. These consist of:
  o Stimulus: instructions for the first task learners are required to do
  o Interaction: instructions for online interaction between learners, based on their reactions to the first task
  o Some activities in Chapter 4: *Creative interaction* have an additional task which asks students to collaborate to create an output product, e.g. a story or poem.
- Variation: included in some activities if the activity lends itself to other contexts, topics or language focus. This will suggest ways in which the activity could be adapted.

Most of the activities require little preparation, and where role cards are needed, they are given on separate photocopiable pages at the end of the activity. Many of the activities, including those with role cards or instructions that teachers may wish to personalize, can also be downloaded from the dedicated website. Details of this can be found on the inside front cover. Material which is available to download is marked with the symbol ⬉.

Synchronous or asynchronous platforms?

The activities are intended to be either synchronous, i.e. taking place in real time, or asynchronous, with a time delay. When trialling the activities with teachers in different classroom and online environments, we found that most of them can be carried out synchronously or asynchronously. Which mode you choose will partly depend on where in the lesson you wish to use the activity, and whether it is a lengthy activity requiring students to do their own research, for example, or one designed as a quick finish to a lesson. Some activities lend themselves better to one mode or the other and in these cases a note is included in the Outline.

References

Bender, T. (2003) *Discussion-Based Online Teaching to Enhance Student Learning*, Virginia: Stylus Publishing LLC.

Callagher, M. (2008) *How can Student Interactivity be Enhanced through the use of a Blended Learning Approach?* Available online at: http://www.core-ed.org/sites/efellows.org.nz/files/Research_Report_-_Mark_Callagher.pdf. [Last accessed March 2016]

Chen, W. and Looi, C-K. (2007) 'Incorporating online discussion in face to face classroom learning: A new blended learning approach', *Australasian Journal of Educational Technology*, 23(3), pp. 307–326.

Croxton, R. (2014) 'The Role of Interactivity in Student Satisfaction and Persistence in Online Learning', *MERLOT Journal Of Online Learning And Teaching*, Vol. 10, No. 2, June 2014, pp. 314–324.

Frazee, R. (2003) 'Using Relevance to Facilitate Online Participation in a Hybrid Course', *Educause Quarterly*, 4, pp. 67–69.

Haugsbakk, G. and Nordkvelle, Y. (2007) 'The Rhetoric of ICT and the New Language of Learning: a critical analysis of the use of ICT in the curricular field', *European Educational Research Journal*, 6(1), pp. 1–12.

Hill, J. R., Song, L. and West, R. E. (2009) 'Social learning theory and web-based learning environments: A review of research and discussion of implications', *American Journal of Distance Education*, 23(2), pp. 88–103.

Liu, X., Magjuka, R. J., Bonk, C. J. and Lee, S.-H. (2007). 'Does sense of community matter? An examination of participants' perceptions of building learning communities in online courses'. *Quarterly Review of Distance Education*, 8(1), pp. 9–24.

Morris, L. V., Finnegan, C. and Wu, S.-S. (2005) 'Tracking student behavior, persistence, and achievement in online courses', *The Internet and Higher Education*, 8 (3), pp. 221–231.

Muirhead, B. (1999) *Attitudes towards Interactivity in a Graduate Distance Education Program: A Qualitative Analysis*. Available online at: http://www.dissertation.com/library/1120710a.htm (p.11)

Ng, C. S. L. Cheung, W. S. (2007) 'Comparing face to face, tutor led discussion and online discussion in the classroom', *Australasian Journal of Educational Technology*, 23(4), pp. 455–469. Available online at: http://ajet.org.au/index.php/AJET/article/view/1246/618. [Last accessed March 2016]

Roblyer, M. and Ekhaml, L. (2000) *How Interactive are your Distance Courses? A Rubric for Assessing Interaction in Distance Learning*. Available online at: http://www.westga.edu/~distance/roblyer32.html. [Last accessed March 2016]

Tello, S. F. (2007) 'An analysis of student persistence in online education', *International Journal of Information and Communication Technology Education*, 3(3), pp. 47–62.

Wagner, E. D. (1994) 'In support of a functional definition of interaction', *The American Journal of Distance Education*, 8(2), pp. 6–29.

Wagner, E. D. (1997) 'Interactivity: From agents to outcomes' in T. E. Cyrs (ed.), *Teaching and learning at a distance: What it takes to effectively design, deliver, and evaluate programs*, San Francisco: Jossey-Bass Publishers.

Further reading

Ally, M. (2004) 'Foundations of Educational Theory for Online Learning' in Anderson, T. and Elloumi, F. (eds.) *Theory and Practice of Online Learning*, Athabasca University, Athabasca: Canada. Available online at: http://cde.athabascau.ca/online_book/ch1.html [Last accessed March 2016]

Andrisani, D., Gaal, A., Gillette, D., and Steward, S. (2001) 'Making the Most of Interactivity Online', *Technical Communication*, 48(3), pp. 309–323.

Mayes, T. (2006) 'Theoretical Perspectives on Interactivity in e-learning', in Juwah, C. (ed.) *Interactions in Online Education*, New York: Routledge.

McCarthy, M. (2016) *The Cambridge Guide to Blended Learning for Language Teaching*, Cambridge: Cambridge University Press.

Payne, C. (2007). 'What do they Learn?' in Khan, B (ed.), *Flexible Learning in an Information Society*, pp.135–145. London: Information Science Publishing.

Thurmond, V. Wambach, K. (2014) 'Understanding Interactions in Distance Education: A review of the literature', *International Journal of Instructional Technology and Distance Learning*, Jan 2004.

1   Setting up and managing online interaction

Once you have got an online space where learners have the possibility of interacting, how do you get started? In some cases, students may spontaneously begin sending messages to the teacher and each other but in our experience this is very rarely the case. Making time for interacting online in a foreign language is challenging. First of all, it will often take learners longer to write something in English than in their own language. Secondly, even though for many people writing into an online platform is easier than speaking, it still can be a bit intimidating for some, especially if they worry that their peers or teacher will criticize or not understand them. Thirdly, your online course is just one of several other online outlets crying for their attention. In the same space as your course, you are competing with work or school emails, messages from friends and family, notifications from various apps, YouTube videos, social media platforms, and in many cases video games too.

However, it *is* possible for interaction to develop and flourish in an online language course. The experience can be productive and rewarding for both the participants and the teacher. It does stand a better chance if you take certain steps, however, both at the beginning of a course and during the course itself. But first of all, you need to make sure that you have the right tools for the job.

Platform considerations

For the purposes of this chapter, we will refer to any area online where interaction can take place as a platform. This may be a social media site, such as Facebook, LinkedIn or Google+. It may be a group in a messaging service such as WhatsApp or Snapchat. It may be a simple discussion forum, on a site such as Yahoo Groups or Proboards. It may be a videoconferencing platform such as Blackboard Collaborate or Adobe Connect. Finally, it may be a virtual learning environment such as Moodle, Edmodo or Canvas.

Whatever platform you use, in order to do many of the activities we propose in the book, at a minimum you need to have a way in which:

- you can communicate publicly via writing or speaking to the students
- the students can communicate publicly via writing or speaking to each other
- you and the students can send private messages to each other
- you and the students can post different kinds of media (at least images, if not video and audio).

All the services we mentioned in the previous paragraph allow you to do these four things. Beyond that, there are other questions to keep in mind if you are choosing a platform to use for online interaction. We have put these together as a checklist of questions. Since web services are changing all the time, we have elected not to list what individual platforms are able to do. It is our hope that this list can help you decide the merits or demerits of any platform you choose to use.

Access and ease of use
- How easy will it be for students to access the platform?
- How familiar are students with the platform already?
- Is it easy to find new and unread messages?
- Is it easy and intuitive to post messages to the group?
- Is it easy to post private messages to each other?

Choosing a new and unfamiliar platform will make it necessary to spend considerably more time preparing instructions and a guide for students to read beforehand, but once it has started they are perhaps more likely to view it as an exclusive English learning space.

Choosing a familiar platform to use (e.g. a Facebook group or Google+ group) will make it much easier to get in, but some students may feel that those spaces are for personal use rather than English language use.

Forum and written message considerations
- Can you create multiple topics?
- How easy is it to start a new topic, and differentiate it from the one that came before?
- Is it possible and easy to upload images and video?
- Is it possible to 'pin' a topic or forum to the top of the page so it will always be easy for participants to find?
- Is it possible to view a discussion in a threaded manner, i.e. with messages and replies grouped together? See Figure 1.1 for an example. Or is it linear, with each message following the other?
- Is it possible for learners to edit and/or delete their posts?
- Is there an optional 'like' button for posts, that you can simply click on to show approval?

Subject	Sender	Date
⊖ My Coat of Arms	Brian Garner Jr.	12-07-2016
├ Re: My Coat of Arms	Nicola Kowalski	12-07-2016
├ Re: My Coat of Arms	Brian Garner Jr.	12-07-2016
└ Re: My Coat of Arms	Russ White	12-07-2016
⊖ Coat of Arms of my family!	Nicola Kowalski	13-07-2016
├ Re: Coat of Arms of my family!	Russ White	13-07-2016
└ Re: Coat of Arms of my family!	Lindsay Clandfield	13-07-2016

Figure 1.1: Example of threaded discussion

We would say that a good platform for interaction answers 'yes' to almost all the above questions.

Videoconferencing considerations
- Does the platform allow participants to post messages in a chat window?
- Is it possible to share slides, images, videos and external websites?

- Is it possible to send students to online 'breakout' rooms where they can discuss something in smaller groups in private?
- Are there tools that allow students the chance to participate non-verbally in a webinar (e.g. a 'raise your hand' button, emoticons, buttons to vote or poll on topics)?
- Can multiple participants speak and/or use video at once?

We would say a good platform answers 'yes' to all these questions as well, with the exception of the final one. At the time of writing, videoconferencing with large numbers of participants is often difficult and impractical due to bandwidth issues. Having lots of people using video and audio at the same time will often, in our experience, lead to slow or distorted sound quality and video quality. Participants with a weak internet connection might find it does not work at all. For this reason, many of the activities in this book can be done with a videoconferencing tool requiring only one person to be on video and audio (and the others participating by writing in a chat window). Of course, if you do have the capabilities to have multiple people on video and audio at once then all the better!

At the beginning of your course

The first few days and weeks of the course are probably the most crucial time to set the stage for interaction to occur. This is the time when expectations for the course can be established and the first encounters online between participants and the teacher will occur.

Getting familiar with the platform

This should be the first order of business. Even if you are using a platform that you think the majority of your students will be familiar with, it is still useful to explain to the students exactly how you expect it to be used during this course. Firstly, students should know how to access the platform. They should know how and where to find tasks, and how and where to post. They should know how to reply to each other online publicly, and how to send private messages to each other and the teacher.

It may be a good idea to prepare a document explaining step-by-step how to do each of these things. This can be sent via email to participants before they start the course, along with a welcome message. Make your instructions clear and in point-by-point fashion. See the example of clearer instructions in Figure 1.2.

Writing Instructions for accessing a course

Unclear instructions:
To get into our forum, just go to the Lefora website and sign up. Then request to join our group. I will authorize your request and you will find the tasks in our forum there.

Clearer instructions:
To get into our forum, follow these steps.
1   Go to Lefora.com and click on 'Sign up'.
2   Follow the instructions on screen to make an account. They will send you a confirmation email with a link so you can then enter.
3   When you have entered, click on the 'Request to join a course' button in the top left corner. A list of courses will appear.
4   Find our course 'English Interaction'. Click on the 'Join' button.
5   I will get a message asking to let you in. I will respond and you will get an email message saying that you are now in the course. Our course will be visible to you on the main page now when you log into Lefora.
6   Click on the course to enter. At the top there is a forum that says 'Welcome'. Open that forum and follow the instructions inside. Congratulations! You have done your first task.

Figure 1.2: Example of instructions

Even more effective is including screenshots of key moments (e.g. Figure 1.3). Making this document will initially take time, but when you have done it once you can use it again and again for other courses.

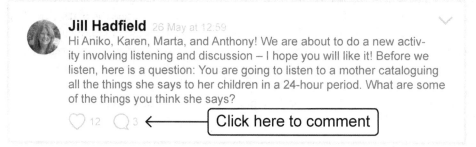

Figure 1.3: Example of annotated screenshot explaining how to comment on a task

Another possibility is to make a video screencast of yourself showing key elements of the platform. You will need screencasting software to do this and a place to upload it but it may be a lot easier for learners to understand what to do if you can actually show them.

Despite your best intentions, there may be some people who still find it difficult to join. This is perfectly normal, so don't worry! They may need you to explain key instructions to them again, or they may just need to start again. It may be that you need to schedule a Skype call or phone call to help certain individuals. You can also ask more experienced students to help out their peers. If you are doing a blended course, it may mean helping someone to log in and get set up in class.

Setting rules for engagement

If you are setting tasks for learners which require them to interact with each other, especially in a foreign language, it is probably a good idea to go over some basic guidelines for the kind of online behaviour you want to see in the forums. Online discussion forums and chat rooms in non-educational contexts are notorious for being places where people get angry, upset and insult each other. Moreover, it is easy to take offence at what someone else has written to you in a public forum when there are no visual cues (smiles, friendly body language) to help you understand that a message may be more in jest than serious. Operating in a foreign language makes it even more likely for messages to be misunderstood or offence to be taken.

It is therefore a good idea to establish basic rules of behaviour in the space where you and your learners will be interacting. These rules are also known as 'netiquette', and any search online will reveal lots of sample guides to netiquette. Figure 1.4 shows a few guidelines that we think are appropriate for a language learning environment.

1 Respect the opinions and views of other people in the forum.
2 Use names when you quote someone, e.g. 'Francis said ...' not 'Someone said ...'.
3 Please do not insult anyone in the forum or use rude language, even as a joke.
4 If you don't think you understand something, ask the person to explain it a different way. You can also send a message to the teacher if you aren't sure.
5 Use appropriate emoticons (smileys, like this ☺) to convey emotion, but don't use too many of them in your messages.
6 You can use common acronyms like LOL (laughing out loud) or TTYL (talk to you later). If you aren't sure that people will understand an acronym, put the meaning in brackets after.
7 Avoid SHOUTING (typing in capital letters) or flaming (getting angry and writing abuse online) in our discussions.
8 If you have a problem with someone in the forum, let the teacher know in a private message.

Figure 1.4: Sample netiquette rules

You can go about establishing these rules in different ways. You could simply post a list of rules for your learners to read and give a task relating to them (e.g. look at the examples of bad behaviour in discussions and match each one to the rule it is breaking). Alternatively, you could negotiate the rules with the learners themselves in one of your early discussions. See Activity 5.15: *Netiquette* for an example of this.

During your course

Some groups of learners on online courses just seem to get off to a good start naturally and interact a lot in course spaces (if there is room for one). Other groups are much quieter and need more guidance and prompting. Either way, there are several interventions that a teacher can stage to help build and sustain interaction.

Have clear instructions for tasks

We touched on the issue of clear instructions for accessing the course, but this advice holds true for any tasks involving interaction that you set within your course. Having clear instructions is something that cannot be stressed enough. Some people will misread or not understand even the easiest of instructions. With unclear instructions an activity may never get off the ground at all, and can end up being a real hindrance to interaction for the rest of the course.

In the activities in this book you will see sample instructions for different stages of all the activities. You can use these as a guide to making your own activities later.

Use names

This is an obvious piece of advice, and one which many face-to-face teachers instinctively know, but it is easy to overlook online. Specifically naming participants in your activities and interactions helps make them feel included as part of the group. Knowing that your name may be mentioned in a group forum is more likely to make you want to come back and check (is anyone talking about me?), and combining a name with judicious praise for a task well done is great for a participant's motivation and self-esteem. Use individual names in setting up tasks, commentary and feedback. It will also help you remember the participants on the course, who can all too easily become 'invisible'.

Encourage participants to post profile pictures

Many online platforms and forums will give you the chance to post a photo of yourself that will appear next to anything you post online (the profile picture). The default image is usually a picture of a blank head (sometimes called a ghost). If learners are on a course which allows them to have a profile photo, it is a good idea to put something there instead of the default image as quickly as possible. If a learner is uncomfortable (for cultural reasons or otherwise) with posting a photo of their face, then tell them they can use another image instead that they would like to represent them, e.g. a flower or a motorcycle – anything that they like and which they feel represents them. Having a profile picture helps you identify each student but more importantly it helps them identify each other.

Lead by example and give praise

At the beginning of a course, most participants will be looking to the teacher for an indication of how, what and when to write. The style of your emails to them, of the announcements in the course and your participation will all help set the tone of what is to follow. It is therefore recommended that you participate more frequently at the beginning of the course, and in a style that you want to be emulated. Bear in mind that just merely reading their posts does not mean that you are participating. Students will not know that you have read a post unless you comment on it, even if this is simply 'liking' the post. So, post early and often at the beginning. You can always reduce your participation later once the group is interacting.

Give generous praise and encouragement early on. If the platform is new to the students, many of them may complete tasks without knowing if they have done it correctly or in the right place. It is important to make them feel comfortable and confident in the course as quickly as possible, and praise can help achieve that. Some useful phrases for giving online praise in forums and chats can be found in Figure 1.5.

Online praise and encouragement

Thanks (*name*) for your contribution here. It was very useful.
Congratulations to everyone for completing this task.
Well done (*name*), you're the first to post. Thanks for getting us started!
Great! You have found the forum and made your first post!
Thank you (*name*), for your answers. I recommend that everyone look at what (*name*) wrote, it's very good.

Figure 1.5: Useful phrases for online praise

While all of this is important, we advise against posting a reply to every single post at the beginning of a course. This can have the unfortunate effect of you having a series of one-to-one public conversations with learners who are not interacting with each other.

Synchronous or asynchronous activities?

Synchronous activities are those in which all participants are communicating at the same time, in real time. Typical examples include a chat room or a videoconference. Asynchronous activities are those in which participants complete a task in their own time. Typical examples include a system of messages or a discussion forum.

Most online courses will have an asynchronous element to them, perhaps with the occasional synchronous task. There is no single right way to balance synchronous and asynchronous tasks, and both have their advantages and disadvantages. Synchronous tasks are usually good for creating or maintaining a sense of group cohesion and getting to know each other. They can be very motivating, but will often lack depth. Also, if your students are distributed over a wide geographical area and live in different time zones, synchronous tasks may not always be feasible. Asynchronous tasks allow for more reflection and planning time. They can foster more language production and lead to deeper and more memorable interaction and learning experiences. However, it is easier for students to avoid participating in an asynchronous task, and there is a risk of discussions going off topic and becoming hard to follow.

In this book we will show examples of both synchronous and asynchronous activities. Some tasks are better suited for synchronous platforms, others for asynchronous platforms. The majority of the tasks can be done either way with small adjustments.

Using deadlines
We have found that, in terms of asynchronous activities, having clear tasks with deadlines helps in maintaining momentum on a course. Having an achievable deadline means that everyone knows when they need to do their part. However, the problem with deadlines is that sometimes it means that people will leave it to the last minute before doing the work. If the task involves interaction and everyone waits until the very end, then there is not much time to interact!

One solution is to have different deadlines for stages of a task. An example would look like the following:

1   Set an initial task for everyone to write something. Set a deadline.
2   Once the deadline is reached, ask the participants to make at least one comment on what another person has written and reply to comments on what they have written. Set a new deadline.

Many of the activities we have included in this book have different stages organized in this way.

Nip problems in the bud

If there are communication problems online, especially in a foreign language course, it is quite likely that participation and interaction will drop very quickly. To prevent this from happening, keep an eye out for problems and address them quickly. Typical problems include the following:

• posting an answer in the wrong place
• accidentally posting something twice or misunderstanding the instructions for a task
• not participating at all
• dominating the conversation and posting far too much
• getting sidetracked from the task at hand
• posting with very inaccurate language that makes understanding difficult
• flaming (insulting or hostile interaction between members).

For any of these, or other problems, it is a good idea to intervene before it becomes a major problem. Sometimes this could take the form of a gentle reminder to everyone in the group through a public announcement. In other cases, it may be best to send a private message to the participant to try and sort out the problem. While it may not always be possible, having a quick live phone call (or Skype call) with a participant about the problem can save lots of time and emails (see *Managing the teacher's time* below).

Teacher interventions during tasks

If a discussion has started and then suddenly begins to wane, one way to reactivate it is to post a summary of what has been said and adjust the task to allow participants another way to come into the discussion. If you do this, use names, praise to those who have participated and encourage the others again to do the original task or a variation. See Figure 1.6 for a sample summary done mid-way through a discussion.

A mid-discussion summary

The original task was to post a description of your family.
Thanks everyone so far for your descriptions! I see a lot of us come from big families. Sarka has six brothers and sisters, and Jordi said he has more than twenty cousins. Many of us have family members in other countries. Jennifer has a brother in Canada, and so does Laurel. I loved some of the family photos, especially the photo of Stephanie's cat!
I look forward to seeing everyone else's descriptions. If you like, you can just choose ONE part of your family, or you can talk about a family pet.

Figure 1.6: Sample summary

Another way to energize a group during a task is to take part yourself, either by playing a different role or simply sharing your own information. Again, you have to be careful that not all interaction ends up going between individual participants and yourself, but intervening with praise, further points and encouraging questions can go some way in re-igniting participation in an online forum.

Wrapping up activities

When you finish an activity that required learner interaction, there are a few things you can do to help maintain or even deepen participant interaction in future activities. Start by declaring the activity over and thanking everyone for their participation. Depending on the activity, you might want to post a summary of what people said (as in Figure 1.6, but now for the end); again, use names here. Everyone likes to see their name 'in lights' on a forum. The summary can be a paragraph or it can be in another form. Other ways we have seen online teachers achieve the same goal include:

- 'top 10' (or 12, or 20) points made in the activity, posted in list form
- series of quotes taken from the activity and put into an animated video
- mind map or word cloud showing visually the main points made
- slide show displaying main points, accompanied by music
- video of you talking through some of the points made and summarizing them
- screencast of the activity, with you highlighting points and discussing them.

Deciding which type of summary to use will depend on the activity, the time you have and your digital skills.

At the end of the activity you may find it worthwhile to give feedback or ask participants to comment on and evaluate the activity or their own participation. We deal with this issue in more detail in Chapter 7: *Feedback and assessment*.

End your wrap-up by giving participants a sense of having achieved something. This can be achieved by the summary, or by restating the aims of the activity. Then finish on a positive note. In our experience online it never hurts to give extra praise!

Managing the teacher's time

Including more interaction in an online course means more teacher time online. Answering messages, prodding inactive members, giving feedback and summarizing are all time-intensive activities, especially so if you are new at this. In addition, it is all too easy to get into a situation in which the teacher is constantly posting or answering student questions. Here are some further tips on how to manage teacher time:

- Make expectations clear. Let students know at the beginning of a course when you will be checking in and when you will not be online. For example, you may wish to tell them that you do not check your work email at weekends, but will get back to them on the Monday morning. You should also let them know more or less how long it will take you to respond to an email or query. We generally advise students that we will respond within 12 hours. Finally, let students know if you are going to be absent for a day or two, or away for a longer time.
- Do not respond to every single post made by students. While it is important to encourage students by responding to what they write, we advise against responding to every post. Instead, we suggest posting a response to two or three student posts, with some brief words or a summary.

- Set up a scheduled 'office hour' time every week. Instead of answering all emails at all times, schedule and announce a designated time or times each week as your office hour. This could mean that you address course-related emails then, or that you are online live in a chat room or videoconference room.
- Create a 'Student questions' discussion thread, where students can post 'off task' questions about other topics. This has the advantage that other students (who may be having the same problem) can read your response, or even that students can answer the questions of their classmates.
- Set tutorials for individual students. Make a list of times and ask students to sign up for short (15-minute) tutorials. These can then be done on Skype or in a chat room. Explain that during the tutorials you can address any individual concerns the student has.

Setting up and managing complex activities

Some activities in the book are more complex than others. This is because they may involve any of the following:

- several stages
- role play with an initial scenario
- stimulus texts to be read, understood and perhaps responded to before the interactive activity
- a mixture of private messaging and open forum
- a higher cognitive demand on the student, for example the requirement to solve a puzzle or to produce a piece of creative writing.

Examples of these are Activity 4.9: *Number plate story*, 6.12: *Rumour mill* and 6.13: *Disappearing act*.

Although these activities are more demanding, they are well worth doing with the students for several reasons. Students will often gain a high level of enjoyment from the very complexity of these activities.

Finally, the challenge and complexity of the activity has the potential to produce more complex and creative exchanges. Figure 1.7 is an example from Activity 6.12: *Rumour mill*.

Alain
I heard that Susie is a party animal but this is definitly not true she is a nice sober nurse

Marian
Who told you she was nice and sober?

Alain
Herself, so maybe it is a lie...

Figure 1.7: Example of interaction from Activity 6.12: *Rumour mill*

Figure 1.8 is an example from Activity 4.9: *Number plate story*.

Pedro

When he was young, Jack met a materialist girl named Maria. Despite all his true love he did not had enough money to satisfy her. Then, the cold hearted girl left him to live a happy life with a richer man, breaking the heart of the poor young Jack.

Emotionally perturbed by this break up Jack became obsessed by money and his revenge, so he worked very hard to earn as much money as possible in order to ruin Maria's husband an buy all their belongings. Currently, Jack is laughing diabolically while driving his big black Maserati decorated by a vanity plate where we can read "WAS HIS".

Figure 1.8: Example of interaction from Activity 4.9: *Number plate story*

Students will often surprise themselves by what the challenge enables them to achieve. This leads to self-esteem and motivation, as well as to enjoyment.

Complex activities need careful setting up and monitoring. They can be done in either synchronous or asynchronous format (of the examples shown, *Number plate story* was done asynchronously and *Rumour mill* synchronously), but you may find the asynchronous format works better to keep the momentum of the activity going. In either case you will need to be tight with deadlines and be prepared to monitor the activity. A few hints and tips:

- Set up the initial scenario or preparation activity very clearly and make sure everyone understands before going on to the next stage, perhaps by asking checking questions.
- If the momentum of the activity relies on students posting stimuli, as for example in Activity 6.6: *Murder mystery*, where each student has a numbered clue which they post in order, make sure that the students are clear about the order of posting and monitor to make sure that a student does not hold the activity up by neglecting to post – remind them by messaging, or step in and post the clue yourself.
- If students communicate one-to-one by private message as in *Rumour mill*, you may want to ask them to include you as a recipient in the messages, in order to check that everything is going smoothly and to be able to provide later feedback and error correction (also to share the fun!).
- If students have put a lot of effort into the activity and produced good contributions, you may like to reward effort with a prize giving or certificate!

2 Personal interaction

2.1 Welcome to the forum

Outline	Students introduce themselves in a forum, and are then assigned a partner to ask questions.
Level	Beginner and above (A1–C1)
Learning focus	Describing yourself, introductions
Time	10–15 minutes per task over three days
Preparation	Make a list of the names of your students and number them.

Procedure

1 Open a forum topic and give it a name (e.g. *Welcome to the forum!*).

2 Post Task 1 and set a deadline for posting answers. If you would like to join in, post an introduction yourself.

Task 1: Stimulus

Welcome to our course! This is your first task. I'd like you to post a quick introduction about yourself. Tell us about you: where you are from, what you do, where you live etc. Please also include the answer to ONE of these questions:

What is your favourite place in the whole world?

What are your two most precious possessions?

What is something that you are very proud of?

Post your answers by *(insert deadline)*.

Please post these as replies to this post. Don't reply to anybody else's post right now, just answer the questions, OK?

---

3 When all students have posted, thank them and then post Task 2. Make sure you include the numbered list of names. If you are going to join in this task, include your own name. Set a deadline for posting questions and replies.

▶ Task 2: Interaction

Thanks everyone! Now read what the others in the group posted. Then look at the list of names below. Find the name of the person BELOW you. You are going to ask that person two or three questions about their introduction. Please do this by replying to their introduction post.

(insert numbered list of names)

Check back to the forum often. If someone asks you a question about your introduction, please answer them as a reply to their question.

If you are the last person on the list, then you ask the first person on the list.

Please post your questions by *(insert deadline)*. All questions should be answered by *(insert deadline)*.

---

4   At the end of the activity, thank everyone for participating. A possible follow-up could be to use some of the facts from this forum to make a true/false quiz to do with the group during a live session.

2.2 A sense of adventure

Outline	The teacher posts a picture of an extreme sport. Students post their reactions and say whether they would do that sport and why. Then they find their own pictures and post with an account of their feelings about that sport. At the end, they decide who is the most/least adventurous student in the class.
Level	Elementary and above (A2–C1)
Learning focus	*would*, vocabulary for emotions, sports
Time	10–15 minutes per task over a week
Preparation	Find a picture of someone doing an extreme sport such as bungee jumping or skydiving.

Procedure

1 You can do this stage face-to-face or online. Show the class the picture and ask them a few questions about it, such as:

Imagine you are the person in this picture. How would you feel?

Think of three words to describe your reaction to this picture.

Would you do this sport? Why? Why not?

2 Set up a forum and give it a name (e.g. *A sense of adventure*). Post Task 1 and set a deadline for posting pictures and explanations.

⬆ Task 1: Stimulus

Find a picture of a sport or activity you would or would not like to do, e.g. climbing, skydiving or kitesurfing. Post your picture together with an explanation of why you would/wouldn't like to do it. Here is an example:

This is a picture of skydiving. I would love to do this one day. I think it would be wonderful to see the views and have the feeling of freedom.

Or

This is a picture of mountain climbing. I would hate to do this. I am not a very brave person and I do not like heights!

Post your picture and explanation by *(insert deadline)*. Do not reply to anybody else's posts at the moment. It's okay if you choose the same sport as someone else.

---

3 When everyone has posted, post Task 2 and set a deadline for posting comments.

> ### ⬛ Task 2: Interaction 1
>
> Now look at other people's pictures. Choose three to comment on. You can either agree with the person, e.g.:
>
> *I agree! I would love to do skydiving too one day. It must be so exciting!*
>
> Or disagree and try to persuade them, e.g.:
>
> *Ali, I don't agree – mountain climbing would be wonderful. Think about the views and the great feeling when you reach the top!*
>
> If a post already has three comments, choose another post.
>
> Post your comments by *(insert deadline)*.

4   While people are commenting, create a list of all the sports posted. When the deadline for Task 2 has passed, post Task 3.

> ### ⬛ Task 3: Interaction 2
>
> Here is a list of all the sports you talked about.
>
> *(insert list here)*
>
> Read the list and answer the following question for each one: *Would I do this sport?* Then count the number of times you answered *Yes*. Post your score as a reply to this message. Who is the most adventurous in the group? Who is the least adventurous?

5   When everyone has posted their score, thank students for their participation and discuss with the group how adventurous (or not) everyone is.

Variation

Instead of sports, you can change this activity so it is about other 'adventurous' things to do. Here are some ideas:

* unusual foods you would eat (e.g. alligator, grasshoppers, strange fruits, brains)
* unusual or adventurous holidays (e.g. visiting the South Pole in Antarctica, horse riding in Mongolia)
* unusual or adventurous jobs (e.g. high-rise window cleaner, war correspondent, cruise line worker).

2.3 A year in the life

Outline	Students are each allocated a year by the teacher and share moments from history and their own lives for that year. They then create a historical quiz for each other based on all the facts they have read.
Level	Elementary and above (A2–C1)
Learning focus	Past simple
Time	10–15 minutes per task over a week
Preparation	No advance preparation required.

Procedure

1   This stage can be done face-to-face or online but in each case should be private – by private message online or by a card given to each student face-to-face.

Allocate each student in your group a year (e.g. 2001). The years you choose should begin sometime after your youngest student was born so that he/she will be able to remember something from that year. Allocate each student a different year, e.g. Student 1: 1999, Student 2: 2001. If you have a large group, divide into smaller groups/forums: probably about 5–6 maximum in a group is ideal for this activity.

2   Set up a forum and give it a name (e.g. *A year in the life*). Post Task 1. Ask students to post their year and two pieces of information: one historical and one personal. Set a deadline for posting replies. Participate yourself in the activity if you have a small group, perhaps by posting the first example about yourself.

Task 1: Stimulus

Post the year I assigned you, together with two pieces of information: one historical event that happened that year, and one sentence about one thing you did that year.

Post your replies by *(insert deadline)*.

---

3   When all replies are in, post Task 2 and set a deadline for posting comments and replies.

Task 2: Interaction

Read what your colleagues wrote. Choose two different people and ask a question or leave a comment, e.g.:

Pierre, why did your family move in 2003? Where were you before? Did you like Paris?

Comment and reply to questions by *(insert deadline)*.

---

4   When all comments and replies are in, put students in pairs and assign Task 3. Set a deadline for posting the quizzes.

Task 3: Historical quiz

Now work in pairs. Read through the posts and comments. Create a historical quiz of five questions. Include historical facts and personal facts about your colleagues, e.g.:

In what year did Pierre's family move?

When was the big tsunami in Japan?

Communicate with each other by private message or email to create your quiz. When you have finished, post your quiz by *(insert deadline)*.

When all the quizzes are posted, choose another quiz and answer the questions from memory. How many did you get right?

---

5   At the end of the activity, thank students for their participation and congratulate those who scored the highest in the quizzes.

2.4 Coat of arms

Outline	Students choose pictures and symbols to create a coat of arms, then ask each other about the reasons for their choice of symbols.
Level	Elementary and above (A2–C1)
Learning focus	Asking about and explaining reasons: *Why ...? Because ...*
Time	30 minutes for Task 1, 10 minutes for Task 2 over a week
Preparation	Find some examples of coats of arms. A search using the terms 'heraldry+symbols+meaning' should yield some examples. This activity requires students to make an image composed of four other images. You may have to show them how to do this using a simple photo editor, or by finding a website for creating a coat of arms using the search terms 'coat of arms + generator'.

Procedure

1 This stage can be done face-to-face or online. Show students some coats of arms, or post them online, explaining that a family coat of arms showed things that were important to the family and the values they held. This was common in mediaeval times but the practice still exists today, for aristocratic families, schools, large organizations, etc.

If necessary, show students how to use a simple picture editor. Alternatively, if you are using a coat-of-arms generator, make sure they know how to use that.

2 Set up a forum and give it a title (e.g. *Coat of arms*). Post Task 1 and set a deadline for students to post their coat of arms.

▶ Task 1: Stimulus

This week you will need to check in to this forum regularly. Create your own coat of arms by choosing four images that symbolize something important to you. Try to choose symbols rather than literal images. For example, if freedom is important to you, you might choose a bird. If success is important, you might choose a star. Arrange these images in the form of a shield and post your shield by *(insert deadline)*.

---

3 When everyone has posted, post Task 2 and set a deadline for posting questions and mottos.

▶ Task 2: Interaction

Choose a coat of arms to ask questions about, e.g. *Did you choose a picture of a bird because freedom is important to you?*

Ask a question to at least three different people about their coat of arms. If three people have already posted questions about a coat of arms, choose a different one. Post your questions by *(insert deadline)*.

Answer any questions about your coat of arms. When you have finished the questions and answers, think of a motto for your coat of arms, e.g.:

Aim for the stars and you will be successful.

Post your motto to the *Coat of arms* forum by *(insert deadline)*.

---

4 Once everyone has finished, you could publish all the coats of arms together using an online curation tool to collect and organize them (search for 'online curation tool' in a search engine), or as a wall display in a classroom.

2.5 Don't you hate it when …?

Outline	Students take turns completing a sentence beginning with *Don't you hate it when …?* or other structures and then suggest alternatives. This activity works better in a synchronous environment.
Level	Elementary and above (A2–C1)
Learning focus	Various informal structures to talk about frustration and other feelings
Time	30 minutes
Preparation	Post an example to illustrate the kind of sentence that can be generated by *Don't you hate it when …?*

Procedure

1   This stage can be done face-to-face or online. Show students your own *Don't you hate it when …?* example, or simply start the class by asking the question to the whole class. Invite them to comment.

2   Set up a chat room or instant message thread and invite your students. Post Task 1 and set a time limit (e.g. 5 minutes) for posting statements.

Task 1: Stimulus

In this activity we're going to take turns talking about situations that make us frustrated. We will always begin with the words *Don't you hate it when …?* Look at the following examples:

Don't you hate it when you open a can of soup and the lid falls in?

Don't you hate it when you set your alarm clock for 7 pm instead of 7 am?

Don't you hate it when the lift stops at every floor, and nobody gets in?

Now everyone post your own *Don't you hate it when …?* statement. Post your statement in *(insert time limit).*

---

3   Respond to students' posts as they come up with encouragement. Make sure students come up with grammatically correct statements, either by rewriting them or encouraging students to correct them.

4   Once everyone has posted, post Task 2 and set a time limit for posting suggestions.

Task 2: Interaction 1

Ok, we've talked about things that frustrate us. Let's talk about something else. Look at the sentence below:

Don't you ……………… it when …?

Can someone suggest a word for the gap? Post your suggestion in *(insert time limit).*

---

5   When someone suggests a word (most likely the first thing they will suggest is *love*), post Task 3 and set a time limit for posting statements. Repeat stage 4.

Task 3: Interaction 2

OK, now let's repeat the first activity but with the new word. Everyone post a sentence beginning with:

Don't you (love) it when …?

Post your statement in *(insert time limit)*.

---

6   At the end, thank everyone for their participation. As a follow-up you can ask them to search online for the phrase *Don't you hate it when?* and *Don't you love it when?* to see lots of other funny examples.

Variation

If you repeat this activity, you can use different sentence frames to express the same function, e.g.:

Isn't it weird / funny / bizarre / maddening (etc.) the way …?
Is it just me, or does anyone else find … strange / annoying / weird?

2.6 Finish my sentence

Outline	The teacher provides sentence stems which the students have to finish with their own ideas on the topic of making plans. This activity works better in a synchronous environment.
Level	Beginner and above (A1–C1)
Learning focus	Future with *will* and *going to*, adverbs of probability, time expressions
Time	20–25 minutes
Preparation	Prepare five or six sentence stems about future plans (see example below).

Procedure

1 Set up a chat room and invite your students. Tell students you are all going to do one activity together. They should read carefully and write in the chat box.

2 Post Task 1. The students read the sentence stems, then type in the end of the sentence when you write the cue 'Now write'.

Type the first sentence stem into the chat box and give the cue: *After class I'm going to …
Now write!*

Task 1: Stimulus and Interaction

Complete the sentence with your own ideas:

After class I'm going to … Now write!

---

3 Comment and respond to what the students write.

4 Continue with the other sentences. Make any corrections short in this activity. When you have finished, thank the students and end the class.

Task 1: Additional sentences

Tonight, after dinner, I think I'm going to …

Next week I'm definitely going to …

I'm certainly not going to …

Next summer I probably won't …

Maybe I'll …

Variation 1

Do this activity as an oral activity. Instead of writing the sentence stems, tell students *Listen carefully. I'm going to say the beginning of a sentence. You have to complete the sentence with your own ideas.* Then say the first sentence stem aloud: *After class I'm going to … Go!* Comment and respond as above.

Variation 2
Do this activity as a warmer using one of the sets of prompts below.

The past week
Last weekend I …
Before coming to class today I …
Today I didn't …
This morning I went …
For breakfast today I had …

What's happening now
Right now I'm sitting …
If I look around me I can see …
I'm wearing …
Today I feel …
At the moment I'm feeling…
Right now I can hear …

2.7 Foodies

Outline	Students take turns posting an image of a food or drink they like / don't like and answering questions about it.
Level	Beginner and above (A1–C1)
Learning focus	Food and drink, question forms
Time	10–15 minutes per task over a week
Preparation	Take (or find) a picture of a dish or a drink that you like.

Procedure

1 Set up a forum and give it a title (e.g. *Foodies*). Post your picture of food or drink.

2 Post Task 1 and set a deadline for posting questions.

Task 1: Stimulus

Here is a picture I took of a (dish / food / drink / meal) I had. Everyone has to post one question about this picture. I will answer your questions. You must post your question by *(insert deadline)*. You cannot repeat the same question, so pay attention to what the others have written!

---

3 Answer students' questions as they write them. Make a note of the questions in a separate document, and correct them. When everyone has posted their questions, post Task 2 and set a deadline for posting pictures, questions and answers.

Task 2: Interaction

Here is a list of the questions you asked about my food picture.

(insert list of students' questions)

I have corrected the language in some areas. For the rest of this task, you will each post a picture of food in the forum. This can be something you ate, something you like / don't like or something you made – as long as it's food or drink!

When you have posted a picture, look at the other pictures. Ask questions to at least three other people about their food picture. Use the questions in the list above to help you. If someone asks a question about your picture, post an answer. You have until *(insert deadline)* to do this task. Good luck!

---

4 At the end, post a summary of all the food or drink items that were posted. Ask students to answer one of the following questions:
Which was your favourite picture?
You need to plan a meal for a group of friends. What food or drink would you choose from our task?
If you could only eat two things from this week's pictures what would they be? Why?

Variation

This activity format can be used with many different topics, e.g. favourite item of clothing, favourite book or favourite souvenir.

2.8 My angle on ...

Outline	Students take a picture of an object that means something to them, from an odd angle, or only showing part of the object so that it is difficult to see exactly what it is. Other students ask questions to try and find out what the object is and then ask the owner about its meaning.
Level	Elementary and above (A2–C1)
Learning focus	*Yes/No* questions
Time	10–15 minutes per task over a week.
Preparation	Find a picture of an object of yours taken from an odd angle (optional).

Procedure

1   This stage can be done face-to-face or online. If you like and have time, show students or post a picture of an object of yours taken from an odd angle and get them to ask questions to discover what the object is and its significance to you.

2   Set up a forum and give it a title (e g. *My angle on ...*). Post Task 1 and set a deadline for posting pictures.

⟰ Task 1: Stimulus

Choose an object you own that means something to you. Take a picture of a part of the object or the object from an unusual angle. Try and take the picture so that it is not easy to see what the object is (but not impossible!). Post the picture on the forum by *(insert deadline)*.

---

3   When all pictures are up, post Task 2 and set a deadline for posting questions.

⟰ Task 2: Interaction 1

Look at your classmates' pictures. Choose three and ask questions to try and find out what the object is. The owner can only answer yes or no, e.g.:

Is it made of metal?

Yes, it is.

Do you use it in the kitchen?

No, you don't.

If three people have already asked questions about a particular picture, choose another picture.

Post your questions by *(insert deadline)*. If no one has found the answer by this deadline, the owner should tell people what the picture is.

Students ask questions to try to guess three objects. Make sure students understand that only three people can ask questions about any particular picture. This is to make sure all students have questions to answer.

4   When all owners have given the names of their objects, post Task 3. Students should now ask more personal questions about the three pictures they have chosen. Set a deadline for posting questions and answers.

▶ Task 3: Interaction 2

Now ask a question to the three owners of the pictures. Try and find out more about the object. Use these questions to help you:

Why it is important?

How long have you had it?

Where did you get it?

Was it a gift?

Post and answer questions by *(insert deadline)*.

---

5   When everyone has finished, thank students for their participation and end the activity.

2.9 My place in the family

Outline	Students are grouped according to their place in the family. In their groups, they discuss how that affected them, and then regroup to discuss the different viewpoints. This activity may be sensitive for students who come from a cultural background that explicitly favours a (male) first born, or for students who have had a difficult family relationship. However it can help students who have common problems (e.g. a bossy elder brother or sister) to find common ground with other students.
Level	Intermediate and above (B1–C1)
Learning focus	Family vocabulary
Time	20 minutes for Task 1, 10 minutes for Task 2 and 30 minutes for Task 3 over a week
Preparation	No advance preparation required.

Procedure

1 This stage can be done face-to-face or online. Find out from students what their place in the family is: eldest, middle, youngest, only child or one of twins. Use this as a basis for grouping students for Tasks 2 and 3. Set up a forum and give it a name (e.g. *My place in the family*). Post Task 1, to be done individually as preparation for group discussion, and set a deadline for completing answers.

▶ Task 1: Stimulus

Think about your place in the family. Are you the eldest, middle, youngest, only child or one of twins? Choose at least five of these questions and write an answer. Do not post your answers in the forum, but instead write them in a document.

1 Do you have specific memories of growing up connected to your place in the family?

2 How did your brothers and sisters behave towards you?

3 How did your parents treat you? Was this different from the way they treated older or younger children?

4 If you are an only child, what effect did this have on the way you were brought up?

5 What were the disadvantages of your place in the family?

6 What were the advantages?

7 Has your place in the family had any lasting effect on the way you think and behave?

Complete your answers by *(insert deadline)*.

---

2 When students have had time to think about the questions in Task 1, open up to five separate forums (eldest, middle, youngest, only child or one of twins) and assign students to each according to their position in the family. Then post Task 2 in each forum. Set a deadline for students to complete their discussions and post their comments.

⬆ Task 2: Interaction 1

You are in a group with other people who have the same place in the family as you. Look at the questions from Task 1 and discuss your answers. Use the answers you prepared in Task 1 to start, but comment on what other people say.

You have until *(insert deadline)* to discuss these questions in your group.

---

3   When the deadline is up, regroup the students. If you have a big group you can create smaller groups containing at least one student from each place in the family, (i.e. one eldest, one middle, one youngest and so on). If you have a small group, you can bring everyone into one forum. Post Task 3 and set deadlines for posting summaries and comments.

⬆ Task 3: Interaction 2

Now you are in a group with other people who have a different place in the family from you.

First, post a summary of your discussion. Use these phrases to help you:

I am the … in my family.

In our group we thought …

One big advantage was …

We often had to …

Post your summaries by *(insert deadline)*.

When the summaries are all posted, look through the other posts by people who had a different place in the family. Choose at least two other people's posts and leave a comment. Reply to comments on yours.

You have until *(insert deadline)* to comment on other posts.

---

4   When everyone has finished commenting, thank students for their participation and end the activity.

Variation
Instead of *My place in the family* you could group students in other ways, e.g.:

Where I grew up (city centre, suburbs, town, village, etc.)
My name (named after a family member, common name, unusual name, foreign name, etc.).

2.10 Post a present

Outline	In pairs, students collect some personal information about each other, then select and post a picture of a present they would like to give that person with an explanation of why they chose it. Recipients thank the giver and comment on their post.
Level	Beginner and above (A1–C1)
Learning focus	Personal information, interests, likes and dislikes, adjectives for describing character
Time	15 minutes per task over five days
Preparation	No advance preparation required.

Procedure

1   This stage can be done face-to-face or online. Put students in pairs; if this stage is online, students should communicate in their pairs by private message. Set up a forum and give it a name (e.g. *Post a present*). Post Task 1 and give them a deadline to find out as much personal information as they can about each other's likes and dislikes, interests, ambitions, wishes and hobbies. In class, they could interview each other for 10 minutes each; online, you could set a deadline of the following day. If you like, you could structure this with an initial task.

Task 1: Stimulus 1

You have until *(insert deadline)* to find out as much as possible about your partner. Ask and answer questions with your partner. Make notes under these headings:

Likes and dislikes

Interests and hobbies

Ambitions and wishes

What kind of person is your partner?

---

2   When students have found out about each other, post Task 2 and set a deadline for posting pictures.

Task 2: Stimulus 2

Now you know a little about your partner's likes, interests, hobbies and ambitions. Can you think of a present that would be good for them? This can be an object (e.g. a book) or a voucher (e.g. for film tickets). Find a picture of your present and post it. Explain why you chose that present, e.g.:

This is a voucher for a go-kart race. I chose this for Maria because she says she loves driving and would like to try racing.

Post your picture by *(insert deadline)*.

---

3   When all pictures are posted, post Task 3 and set a deadline for posting replies.

Task 3: Interaction

Thank your partner for their present and say why you like it! Post your reply by *(insert deadline)*.

---

4   Allow students to thank each other for the presents. When they have finished, collect all the pictures of presents and put them in a new discussion thread or picture collage. Wrap up by posting Task 4 and set a deadline for posting replies. Note that this final task works best if you delete the posts from Tasks 1–3 so that students have to work from memory.

Task 4: Follow-up

Here are all the 'presents' you gave each other in this activity. Can you remember:

- who got which present?

- why?

Post your answers to me in a private message by *(insert deadline)*.

---

5   Collect the answers, and congratulate the student(s) who got the most correct answers. If you have a quiz-making tool (or find one online, using the search terms 'create your own quiz'), you could make stages 3 and 4 into a quiz.

Variation

Instead of making the exchange about presents, make it a holiday that students have to choose for each other. Say where they could go and what kind of holiday (activity, tourism, etc.) they could have.

2.11 Happy picture

Outline	Students post a picture of a scene or object that means happiness for them. They ask each other questions about their pictures and the meaning and answer them.
Level	Elementary and above (A2–C1)
Learning focus	Question forms, discussing what happiness means to students
Time	10–15 minutes per task over three days
Preparation	No advance preparation required.

Procedure

1   This stage can be done face-to-face or online. Ask students:
   What makes you happy? Think of a happy moment you had recently. (for elementary students)
   Is happiness something you work for or is it something that happens unexpectedly?
   Is happiness a permanent state or is it found in small moments?

2   Set up a forum and give it a title (e.g. *Happy picture*).

3   Post Task 1 to all students. Set a deadline for posting pictures.

Task 1: Stimulus

What is your definition of happiness? What makes you happy? Find a picture that expresses the feeling of happiness to you, or that helps you remember a happy moment. It can be one of your own pictures, or a picture online. Post it by *(insert deadline)*.

---

4   After the deadline is up, post Task 2 and set deadlines for posting and replying to questions. You could join in by asking some questions yourself on different pictures.

Task 2: Interaction

Look at three other people's pictures and post a question about their pictures, e.g.:

Did you post this picture because …?

Do you have a special memory connected with the picture?

Can you explain why ….?

(If any picture already has three questions, choose another picture.)

Post your questions by *(insert deadline)*.

When your picture has three queries, reply to the questions. Reply by *(insert deadline)*.

---

5   At the end of the activity, ask for a volunteer to take all the pictures and make a single picture collage entitled 'Happiness'.

Variation

If you repeat the activity, you could use one or more of the following topics instead of happiness:

- friendship
- love
- holidays
- success
- education
- adventure

2.12 This or that?

Outline	Students write pairs of options and then ask and answer questions using degrees of emphasis to choose one of the options and find out each other's preferences. This activity works better in a synchronous environment.
Level	Beginner and above (A1–C1)
Learning focus	Using emphasis to agree, expressing preferences
Time	15 minutes
Preparation	No advance preparation required.

Procedure

1 This stage can be done face-to-face or online. Teach the following ways of agreeing from emphatic to weak:

Definitely! (emphatic)
For sure!
Absolutely.
Yes.
I guess.
I suppose. (weak)

2 Set a time and meet your students in a chat room. Post Task 1.

▶ Task 1: Stimulus

I'm going to write two things. You need to choose which one you prefer. Write the name of the thing you prefer and use one of the expressions we learned before.

For example, I write:
Travelling by bus or travelling by train?

You write:
Travelling by train, absolutely!

If you don't like travelling by bus and you don't like travelling by train you can write:
Neither!

Ready? Let's start.
Travelling by bus or travelling by train?

---

3 Let students write their answers. Then give another choice of two things (see the list at the end of the activity for ideas). Help with any unknown vocabulary. After they have done a few examples, post Task 2.

⬛ Task 2: Interaction

Now it's your turn. Think of two things that are different, but related.

The first person who is ready can post their two things.

The next person responds, then posts their two things, e.g.:

A: *Bus or train?*

B: *Bus, definitely! Cats or dogs?*

C: *Cats for sure. Lasagne or pizza?*

And so on.

Start when you're ready!

---

4   Let the next stage continue for 5–10 minutes. If there are some gaps between posts because students are having difficulty in thinking of ideas, you could join in yourself. See ideas below.

5   Bring the activity to an end and thank the group. Make a list of all the things listed in the game and use this for future review.

Sample pairs of options
- cats or dogs?
- lasagne or pizza?
- chocolate ice cream or strawberry ice cream?
- the mountains or the beach?
- city or country?
- American English or British English?
- football or basketball?
- books or cinema?
- sparkling water or still water?
- tea or coffee?

2.13 *Yum* or *Yuck?*

Outline	Students take turns posting a name or description of a food item or dish and then react to each other's dishes. This activity works well in a synchronous environment.
Level	Beginner and above (A1–C1)
Learning focus	Food and drink, *Do you like …?*
Time	15 minutes
Preparation	Have a list of a few food dishes ready that are appropriate for your students in language level, but that you are sure will provoke different reactions (i.e. that some people may like and others may not). See suggested examples below.

Procedure

1 Greet students in a chat room and explain the two words *yum* and *yuck*. Both are informal words used by people (often children) to describe food. *Yum* is a positive reaction to something, usually food (also *yummy*) while *yuck* is used to express strong distaste or disgust.

Post Task 1 and ask students to write *yum* or *yuck* about each dish. If you are working asynchronously, set a deadline for posting replies.

Task 1: Stimulus

I'm going to post a very short description of a dish or a drink and ask you if you like it. Write your answer, either *yum* (you like this) or *yuck* (you don't like it). After you have done this, I'll post a new one and you post your reaction to that. We continue like that. If you don't know what the dish is, then ask.

Please post your reply by *(insert deadline)*.

---

2 Go through your dishes, each time writing *Do you like (name of dish)?* You can respond to students' responses here, for example *Yuck? You don't like it? I love that food!* or *I agree. Spinach. Yuck!*

3 Post Task 2 and let students have a minute to think about their dish. If you are working asynchronously, set a deadline for posting choices.

Task 2: Interaction

Now I want you to think of a dish you can describe in a similar way. I'll start again with a new dish, but when you answer you then post your dish right away. And we continue like that. It should look like this:

Teacher: *Do you like tea with milk?*

Student 1:   *Yum! Do you like fish stew?*

Student 2:   *Yuck! Do you like chocolate chip cookies?*

Student 3:   *Yum! Do you like oysters?*

And so on.

Everyone should reply and post one choice by *(insert deadline)*.

---

4   Begin the activity again, but now allow students to answer each other as well. Join in at times to keep the activity going.

5   When you feel enough time has gone by, end the activity. Depending on your students' level, ask follow-up questions about how they responded, e.g.:
    Which of these dishes do you like best?
    Why don't you like (X)? Have you always liked (X)?
    Are you a picky eater in general or do you like to try new things?

Sample dishes
- iced tea
- chocolate bar with pepper or spice
- peanut butter sandwich
- deep fried chicken
- chocolate chip cookies
- fish stew
- pizza with anchovies
- canned tuna
- goat's cheese

3 Factual interaction

3.1 Stats quiz

Outline	The teacher posts a number of statistical sentence stems (e.g. *20% of people ...*). Students race to complete the statistic. The students post their own statistical starters.
Level	Elementary and above (A2–C1)
Learning focus	Present simple, *will*
Time	10–15 minutes per task over a week
Preparation	Research a number of statistical facts. This can be done simply by entering a percentage into a search engine, e.g. '20% of the people'. The results will give you a number of factual endings, which you can use to check students' answers e.g.:

- *... own 80% of the wealth.*
- *... are highly sensitive.*
- *... will never like you.*
- *... only read headlines and not the whole story.*

Procedure

1 Set up a forum and give it a name (e.g. *Stats quiz*). Post Task 1 and set a deadline for posting responses.

⬚ Task 1: Stimulus

I'm going to post a statistic. Your task is to complete the sentence. Everyone can post only once. Your answer can be researched or a guess!

My statistic:

20% of the people ...

Example reply:

... own 80% of the wealth.

Post your answers by *(insert deadline)*.

---

2 When all answers are in, post Task 2 which asks students to decide whether the statistics are real or a guess. Set a deadline for posting comments and replies.

▶ **Task 2: Interaction 1**

Now comment on other students' replies. Do you think they are real or a guess? You must say why, e.g.:

I think '20% of people own 80% of the wealth' used to be true, but is not true now because the gap between rich and poor is getting bigger. I read an article which said that the richest 1% of people own about 50% of the wealth.

Reply to comments on your own post saying whether you guessed, or found the information by researching!

Comment and reply by *(insert deadline)*.

---

3   When comments and replies are in, post Task 3 which asks students to research and post their own 'statistical starters' and to complete and comment on others' posts in the same way. Set a deadline for posting statistics and replies.

▶ **Task 3: Interaction 2**

Your turn! Look online and find a statistic that can be completed in a number of different ways. You can do this by typing a percentage into a search engine. Post your statistic, e.g.:

30% of people … / 30% of the world … / 50% of animals …, etc.

Now comment on other students' replies. Do you think they are real or a guess?

Reply to comments saying whether you guessed, or found the information by researching!

Post, comment and reply by *(insert deadline)*.

---

4   When everyone has finished, thank students for their participation and end the activity.

3.2 Records race

Outline	Students race to find the answers to various 'world record' questions. This activity works better in a synchronous environment.
Level	Elementary and above (A2–C1)
Learning focus	Superlatives, *Wh-* questions
Time	20 minutes
Preparation	Prepare a list of questions about different world records. These could be a variety of themes, or all based on one theme (e.g. geography). See below for two sets of questions you can use, or devise your own.

Procedure

1   Set up a chat room and invite your students. Then post Task 1.

Task 1: Stimulus

I'm going to ask you a question about a world record. Find the information as quickly as possible. When you find the answer, type it into the chat box.

Ready? Here is the first question.

What is the longest river in the world?

---

2   Allow students to answer. Once over half of them have answered, confirm the correct answer and congratulate them. Then post Task 2.

Task 2: Interaction

Now I'm going to nominate one of you to ask the next question. I will give you only the key words. You must make a correct question from them.

So, for example, if I give you:

What / long / river in the world?

You should write:

What is the longest river in the world?

OK, ready? I'm going to give the first one to *(student's name)*.

---

3   Send a private message with the key words to the student who answered Task 1 correctly first.

4   Repeat stages 2 and 3 until you have finished your questions.

5   Wrap up and thank the students. As a follow-up, you could ask them to write a quiz based on these or other world records.

Sample question sets

Geography (answers in brackets)

1   What is the tallest mountain in the world? *(Mount Everest)*
2   What is the longest river in the world? *(The Nile; although some say the Amazon if you include the delta)*
3   What is the largest country in the world? *(Russia by area, China by population)*
4   What is the smallest country in the world? *(Vatican City by area, South Georgia by population)*
5   What is the most populated city in the world? *(Tokyo)*
6   What is the coldest place in the world? *(Antarctica)*
7   What is the largest island in the world? *(Greenland)*

Other (answers may vary for these)

1   How old is the oldest person in the world?
2   What is the fastest time for a marathon?
3   What country has the fastest internet connection?
4   What day is the longest day of the year?
5   What is the latest smartphone?
6   What is the longest word in the English language?
7   What was the biggest blockbuster film last summer?

3.3 Word association chain

Outline	Students take turns typing a word that is associated in some way with the word above it in the chat room. This activity works better in a synchronous environment.
Level	Elementary and above (A2–C1)
Learning focus	Synonyms, antonyms, topic vocabulary, collocations
Time	15 minutes
Preparation	Make sure your students understand the terms *synonym*, *antonym* and *collocation*.

Procedure

1   Set a time and open a chat room. Post Task 1.

Task 1: Stimulus and Interaction

In this activity, one person starts and types a word. The word has to be a name of something you find in an office.

The next person types a word associated with that word. This can be a synonym, an antonym, a collocation or another word in the same family (e.g. *study, student, studious*) or topic area. It can be a verb, an adjective or an adverb.

The next person types a new word that is associated with the last word typed.

Continue this way until everyone has typed one word.

Here is an example:

tea

India

elephants

memory

seaside holidays

---

2   Nominate a student to start and keep an eye on the activity. When everyone has participated, end the activity by saying *We got from (original noun) to … (final word). How?* Ask questions about the words they chose, e.g.:
Q: *Why are tea and India connected?*
A: *Because lots of tea comes from India.*
Or
Q: *Why did you write 'yellow' after 'red'?*
A: *Because yellow and red are the colours of the Spanish flag.*

3   Repeat the activity if desired, beginning with a different student and a different first word.

3.4 Find a festival

Outline	Students post a picture of a festival in their country held at that time of year. Other students ask questions about the festival. If students are from the same country, or to vary the activity, students could research different countries' (or UN) festivals.
Level	Elementary and above (A2–C1)
Learning focus	Present simple questions
Time	2–3 days
Preparation	No advance preparation required.

Procedure

1 This stage can be done face-to-face or online. Write on the board or post the word *festival*. Brainstorm vocabulary that is associated with this word, e.g.:
verbs: *eat, dance, give, celebrate*
nouns: *fireworks, procession, costume*
adjectives: *colourful, exciting*

2 Set up a forum and give it a name (e.g. *Find a festival*). Post Task 1 with a picture of a festival from your country, if possible held around the time of year of posting. Invite questions. Answer the questions as they come in. If all your students are from the same country, choose a festival from a different country or an international one (e.g. United Nations Earth Day, 22 April). Set a deadline for posting questions.

Task 1: Stimulus

This is a picture of *(name of festival)*. It is held in (season) every year in *(name of country)*.

Ask some questions about this festival and I will (try to!) answer.

Post your questions by *(insert deadline)*.

---

3 Post Task 2 inviting students to post a picture of a festival from their country, an international festival or a festival from another country and ask others to ask questions. Set a deadline for posting pictures.

Task 2: Interaction 1

Now you! Find a picture of a festival from your country, a festival from another country or an international festival. If you can find a picture of you and your family or friends at this festival, that would be nice! Post the picture with the name of the festival and the season it is held.

Then look at everybody's pictures. Choose three and ask questions about the festival.

If three people have already asked questions, choose another festival.

Post by *(insert deadline)*.

---

4   Post Task 3 and ask students to answer any questions they were asked. Set a deadline for posting answers.

Task 3: Interaction 2

Look back at your picture. Answer any questions you have there. At the end of the activity, post which two festivals you would most like to go to, and why. Post by *(insert deadline)*.

---

5   When everyone has finished, thank students for their participation and end the activity. You could follow up this activity with Activity 4.5: *Design a festival*.

3.5 Country facts

Outline	Students race to research and post facts about a country that they are unfamiliar with. They then repeat the activity with another country.
Level	Beginner–Elementary (A1–A2)
Learning focus	Present simple questions
Time	10–15 minutes per task over a week
Preparation	No advance preparation required.

Procedure

1   Choose a country that you think your students will know little about. For example, avoid the country which they come from. Also avoid using well-known English-speaking countries like the USA or UK.

Start a forum and give it a title (e.g. *Country facts*). Post Task 1, using the name of the country you chose. Set a deadline for posting facts.

Task 1: Stimulus

I'm going to give you the name of a country. Everyone has to post at least two facts about this country. You cannot repeat the same facts. You are allowed to post images, but they must be connected to the facts.

Please post your facts by *(insert deadline)*.

Here is the name of the country:

BELIZE

If you want to add a competitive element and/or make sure your students do not cut and paste facts from an online country description, add the following rules to Task 1.

Task 1: Rules

Use your own words! Don't cut and paste.

You get a point for every fact you post.

But if you cut and paste you lose a point!

If you can prove another student has cut and pasted, then you get an extra point!

---

2   When everyone has posted, congratulate them in the forum and write a quick summary of the facts. Make any important corrections as needed.

3   Nominate the first person who posted, and give them Task 2. Set a deadline for posting the name of the country.

Task 2: Interaction

Congratulations! You were the first person to post. Now you can choose the next country. Please choose a country that:
- is not the home country of any student
- is not a famous English-speaking country.

If you choose a small country that we don't know anything about we can all learn something!

Please post your choice by *(insert deadline)*.

---

4   Students now repeat the task. You can join in as well on this one.

5   Repeat stage 3, and continue like this for as many students as you like, have time for, or as long as their interest allows!

6   As a follow-up, use the facts the students came up with to make a simple quiz.

3.6 Online drilling

Outline	The teacher provides a core sentence and then gives prompts. Students need to rewrite the sentence correctly according to the prompt. This activity works better in a synchronous environment.
Level	Beginner and above (A1–C1)
Learning focus	Countries and cities, the verb *to be*
Time	15 minutes
Preparation	This can be done face-to-face or online. Teach and/or review the verb *to be* (affirmative and negative) as well as the words for countries and nationalities in English. You could also prepare some core sentences and a series of prompts for transformation. See *Sentence prompts* below for ideas.

Procedure

1 Set a time and open a chat room. Post Task 1. Use the sentence prompts you have prepared or those below. You could practise only countries, or nationalities, or mix the two for higher-level students.

Task 1: Stimulus

What do you know about geography?

Here is a sentence:

Toronto is in Canada.

Here are more words:

Montreal and Vancouver.

Quickly write a new sentence with those words, e.g.:

Montreal and Vancouver are in Canada.

Now here are new words:

the USA

Change the sentence again, e.g.:

Montreal and Vancouver aren't in the USA.

Ready?

---

2 Go through your sentences and cues for changes (see *Teacher-led sentence prompts* below). Correct when you see errors of form or meaning. After you have worked through your teacher-led examples, set the student-led Task 2. Students can change any part of the sentence they wish – the country, capital city or nationality – but they should only change one of these in each turn. When Student 1 has posted, he/she nominates Student 2 and instructs him/her, and so on.

Task 2: Interaction

Now you!

(Student 1), please begin.

Write a sentence, e.g.:

Moscow is the capital of Russia.

Name another student, e.g.:

(Student 2), please go on.

Student 2 changes the sentence, e.g.:

Moscow isn't the capital of China.

Name another student, e.g.:

(Student 3), please go on.

Student 3 changes the sentence again, e.g.:

Beijing is the capital of China.

Go on until everyone has written a sentence.

---

3 Correct any problems in the sentences that come up. At the end, thank everyone for their participation.

Teacher-led sentence prompts (suggested answers in brackets)
Prompts practising countries
1 Toronto is in Canada.
2 Montreal and Vancouver *(Montreal and Vancouver are in Canada.)*
3 USA *(Montreal and Vancouver aren't in the USA.)*
4 Texas *(Texas is in the USA.)*
5 Europe *(Texas isn't in Europe.)*
6 Spain and Italy *(Spain and Italy are in Europe.)*

Prompts practising nationalities
1 Beijing is a Chinese city.
2 Shanghai *(Shanghai is a Chinese city.)*
3 Tokyo and Osaka *(Tokyo and Osaka aren't Chinese cities.)*
4 Japanese *(Tokyo and Osaka are Japanese cities.)*
5 Russian *(Tokyo and Osaka aren't Russian cities.)*
6 St Petersburg *(St Petersburg is a Russian city.)*
7 Paris *(Paris isn't a Russian city.)*

3.7 Wit and wisdom

Outline	The teacher posts the first half of a witticism. Students race to complete it and find out who said it. They comment, then take it in turns to post the next.
Level	Intermediate and above (B1–C1)
Learning focus	Idiomatic language
Time	2–3 days
Preparation	Research a number of witty comments made by historical or famous people. Some examples are given below.

Procedure

1 This stage can be done face-to-face or online. Ask students to match the beginnings and endings of the quotations you have researched. If online, post them and ask them to race to match them; if face-to-face, you can either give them the task in pairs to match, or give half the class beginnings and half the class endings and ask them to mingle until they find their partner.
    Here are some example quotations (from Oscar Wilde).

Beginnings

1 There is only one thing in the world worse than being talked about …
2 The good ended happily and the bad unhappily.
3 I can resist everything …
4 Experience is the name everyone gives …
5 The basis of optimism is …

Endings

a … except temptation.
b … That is what fiction means.
c … and that is not being talked about.
d … to their mistakes.
e … sheer terror.

Answers: 1c   2b   3a   4d   5e

2 Divide students into two teams and assign a private message or chat room to each team.

3 Post Task 1 with a selection of quotations. Set a deadline for posting complete quotations.

> **▶ Task 1: Stimulus**
>
> Here are the beginnings of a number of famous and witty remarks:
>
> 1   I never hated a man enough to …
>
> 2   By the time a man is wise enough to watch his step …
>
> 3   [He is] a modest man who …
>
> 4   He has no enemies but …
>
> 5   I like long walks …
>
> 6   There is no love sincerer than …
>
> Work in your teams. Find the endings and who made the remark. Which team can post a complete list of the sayings and their authors first? Do not post until you have a complete list. Post your list by *(insert deadline)*.

4   When one team has posted, check the answers and declare a winner.

Here are the full quotations for checking:

1   I never hated a man enough to give his diamonds back. (Zsa Zsa Gabor)
2   By the time a man is wise enough to watch his step he's too old to go anywhere. (Billy Crystal)
3   [He is] a modest man who has much to be modest about. (Winston Churchill)
4   He has no enemies but is intensely disliked by his friends. (Oscar Wilde)
5   I like long walks, especially when they are taken by people who annoy me. (Noel Coward)
6   There is no love sincerer than the love of food. (George Bernard Shaw)

5   Then post Task 2. In this task students work in their teams to find five witty quotations they like and to post the beginnings. Set a deadline for posting sentence beginnings.

> **▶ Task 2: Interaction 1**
>
> Still working in your teams, find five quotations that you like. Post the beginnings for the other team to complete.
>
> Post the beginnings by *(insert deadline)*.

6   Finally, post Task 3. In this task students do not look up the sentence endings and authors, but instead they use their imagination to try to complete the quotations themselves. Set a deadline for posting their own sentence endings and the real ones.

▶ **Task 3: Interaction 2**

When both teams have posted, try to complete the other team's sentences yourselves. Don't look anything up this time! Use your imagination and discuss possible endings in your teams. Decide which ones are the best and post them.

Post your endings by *(insert deadline)*.

When the other team has completed your quotations, post the real answers.

Post by *(insert deadline)*.

---

7 When each team has posted, the teams can reveal the actual endings and the authors. Round off the activity by thanking everyone for their participation.

3.8 Where in the world am I?

Outline	Students look at a picture of a place that you have posted and try to guess where in the world it is.
Level	Elementary and above (A2–C1)
Learning focus	Question forms, prepositional phrases
Time	10–15 minutes per task over three days
Preparation	Choose a place anywhere in the world and find an image of it. Do not use a famous landmark that students might recognize. It could be a house or a landscape – any kind of place as long as you know exactly where it is.

Procedure

1 Set up a forum and give it a name (e.g. *Where in the world am I?*).

2 Post Task 1 with the picture and the rules of the activity. Students should think about the kind of questions they can ask. With lower-level students you could use this stage to check question forms, but do not answer questions until Task 2.

Task 1: Stimulus

Look at the picture. Imagine I took this picture. Where in the world am I? You have to guess where I am. You can only ask yes/no questions, e.g.:

Are you in Europe or Africa? ✗ This is not a yes/no question.

Are you in Europe? ✓

First, think of your questions carefully! Look at the examples below to help you make good questions.

Are you east of ... / north of ... / west of ...?

Is this in a big city / small town / village ...?

Is it a warm / cold / hot / dry place ...?

---

3 Now post Task 2 and set a deadline for students to identify the place. Allow students to ask questions. Only answer *yes* or *no*. Correct or reformulate incorrect questions as they come up. Students can guess when they think they know the answer.

Task 2: Interaction

You have 25 questions to guess where I am. Post your questions in the forum. I will answer them. Be careful! If you ask the same question twice it counts as two questions. So read the other questions and my answers before asking a new question.

You have until *(insert deadline)* to find me. Can you do it? Good luck!

---

4 The first person to guess the place chooses the next place. They post a picture of that place for everyone else (including the teacher) to guess.

5 When everyone has posted a picture, end the activity and thank students for their participation.

3.9 Treasure hunt

Outline	Students look at a map posted on the forum and take it in turns to post directions, each student starting at the end point of the last student's directions. The final student's directions lead to the treasure. The others post the location.
Level	Elementary and above (A2–C1)
Learning focus	Giving directions, prepositions of place
Time	Minimum two days (one to post and one to reply)
Preparation	Find an example map with an obvious start point and a number of named locations. Mark START HERE at a point on the map.

Procedure

1   This stage can be done face-to-face or online. Make copies of the map and hand them out to students, or post the web reference to the map online. Give them directions from the starting point to a location on the map. Ask them to follow and identify the location.

2   Set up a forum and give it a name (e.g. *Treasure hunt*). Choose a location as a starting point (e.g. *You are standing outside the Mezze Café, facing north.*). Assign each student a number. (If you have a large group, make two or more groups with a maximum of six students in each.) Post Task 1 and set a deadline for posting directions (directions below are examples).

Task 1: Stimulus

Look at the map. You are starting from …

Student 1 goes first. Post directions from the Start point to any other location you choose, e.g.:

Clue 1: Turn left. At the first traffic lights turn left again and go straight on. At the next traffic lights, turn left and go straight on. At the second traffic lights, turn right and go straight on. Go into the building at the corner of the street.

Do not name streets or buildings!

Post by *(insert deadline)*.

---

3   When Student 1 has posted directions, post Task 2 and set a deadline for everyone to post directions.

Task 2: Interaction 1

Now read Student 1's directions. Where are you?

Now Student 2 should post directions from that place to another location on the map.

Follow Student 2's directions. Where are you?

Then it is Student 3's turn to post directions. Keep following the directions on the map.

Keep going till everyone in the group has posted. You should all post by *(insert deadline)*.

4　Carry on until every student has posted directions following on from the previous student. When the last student has posted directions, post Task 3 for students to identify the location of the treasure (as decided by the last student to post).

Task 3: Interaction 2

Everyone read all the directions. Where are you? That is where the treasure is hidden. Can you be the first to post the name of the place?

5　Check through the directions yourself. If one of the students in the middle made a mistake in their directions, it is possible the treasure cannot be found! If this is the case, tell the class the treasure remains hidden and repeat the activity.

6　Finish the activity by thanking students for their participation.

3.10 This week's guest ...

Outline	Students interview a guest to the course. They choose different subject areas to ask questions about, and write up a summary at the end.
Level	Intermediate and above (B1–C1)
Learning focus	Question forms, narrative tenses
Time	A week
Preparation	For this activity you will need an English-speaking guest to join your course for a week. This can be a friend, colleague or family member. Ask them to think of three or four events in their life that they would like to be interviewed about by the students.

Procedure

1 Set up a forum and give it a name (e.g. *This week's guest*).

2 Post Task 1: an introduction of your guest and the life events they will answer questions about. Below is an example; you should use your own, real guest's details for the activity.

Task 1: Stimulus

This week we are joined by a friend of mine from Canada. His name is Anthony Eder and he will be taking questions this week. You have to interview him about an aspect of his life.

Here are some interesting things about Anthony:

- He failed his driving test seven times.
- He has a Masters degree from Harvard University, and was there at the same time as Mark Zuckerberg, the founder of Facebook.
- He was a participant in several interesting psychology experiments at university.
- He went to Nepal for six months to do a special research project.

Anthony is happy to answer questions and tell you more about any of these life events!

---

3 Post Task 2 and set a deadline for posting questions, based on the time your guest has available.

Task 2: Interaction

Choose one of these areas and find out more about it. At the end of the week you are going to write a summary of what you found out. Post your questions for Anthony in the forum. He will only be able to answer questions until *(insert deadline)* so it's best to get started soon!

Allow students to ask questions. The guest should post answers. Make a note of any problems for future correction, and intervene only if you think the questions are not understood by the guest.

4 Once the guest has answered the questions during the week, thank him/her. Post Task 3. Students have to write 3–4 paragraphs about the event they asked about in Task 2. Set a deadline for posting summaries.

Task 3: Write-up

Please write a short summary of the event that Anthony told you about. Your composition must be 150–200 words long. It should be in the third person (e.g. *He went to school with Zuckerberg,* not *I went to school with Zuckerberg*). Try to organize the facts in a logical way, and make connections between them, e.g. *After that, he … That's why he … So then he …,* etc.

No copying or pasting allowed. Send me your compositions via email by *(insert deadline)*.

5   Once you have the compositions, correct them as you would any piece of writing and post a summary and thank you to your guest and the students in the forum.

3.11 Tell me about …

Outline	Students take turns posting a topic they would like to know more about. Other students post facts about the topic and the original student decides which fact is most interesting.
Level	Intermediate and above (B1–C1)
Learning focus	Music or any other topic-specific vocabulary
Time	A week
Preparation	No advance preparation required.

Procedure

1 This stage can be done face-to-face or online. Tell students that you want them to think about a kind of music they would like to know more about. Give them an example yourself, e.g. *I'm curious about Cuban music* or *I don't know anything about Chinese pop songs.*

2 Set up a forum and give it a name (e.g. *Tell me about music!*). Nominate a student and assign Task 1. Set a deadline for posting facts. Tell students they must not cut and paste their facts! (If you want to introduce a competitive element, see Activity 3.5 on page 56.)

▶ Task 1: Stimulus

(Student 1), you are going to start. Think of a kind of music you would like to know more about. This could be music from a particular country (e.g. Chinese music, Cuban music, English music), a certain kind of music (e.g. heavy metal, pop, folk) or a specific group or artist.

When you have an idea, please post the following sentence in this forum:

Tell me about (insert your topic here).

When *(Student 1)* has posted their sentence, it's everyone else's turn. Please find one interesting fact about this music and post it as a reply in this forum. Please do this by *(insert deadline)*.

---

3 Students should now all post interesting facts they find online about the music the first student asked about. Check in on the forum to make sure they are all on task.

4 Once all students have posted an answer, nominate the original student and give all the students Task 2 in the forum. Set a deadline for Student 1 to post their response.

▶ Task 2: Interaction

(Student 1), now read your partners' responses. Which fact did you think was most interesting? Copy that fact and say who wrote it. That person now continues the activity. Ask us to tell you about another kind of music!

Please post your response by *(insert deadline)*.

---

5 Repeat stages 2 and 3 until all students have had a turn, or as many students have posted as are able to in the time limit.

6 Finish the activity by thanking students for their participation.

Variation

This activity can be done with many topics, e.g.:

- food (e.g. *Tell me about Thai food / vegan dishes / unusual diets.*)
- cities (e.g. *Tell me about Budapest.*)
- culture (e.g. *Tell me about customs in Bali.*)
- jobs and careers (e.g. *Tell me about being a speech therapist. What does it involve?*)
- films and actors (e.g. *Tell me about Bradley Cooper. / Tell me about Steven Spielberg. / Tell me about the making of 'The Lord of the Rings'.*)

3.12 Sports shorts

Outline	Students write three rules for a sport, which others have to guess.
Level	Elementary and above (A2–C1)
Learning focus	Sports, rules of popular sports
Time	A week
Preparation	Make sure you are familiar with the rules of the sports you assign to students. See the possible list of sports below.

Procedure

1 This stage can be done face-to-face or online. Go over the rules of football/soccer with the students, highlighting key phrases and asking them to help you complete the rules. e.g.:

You play this game … (in two teams).

Each team has … (11 players).

You play this game with … (a ball, and two nets).

You play the game … (on a pitch).

You cannot … (touch the ball with your hands). You have to … (pass and kick the ball with your feet).

To score a goal, you need to … (kick the ball into the opponent's net).

The team with the most … (goals) wins.

2 Set up a forum and give it a name (e.g. *Sports shorts*) and assign each student a sport from the list below. Post Task 1 and set a deadline for posting rules.

▶ Task 1: Stimulus

I have given each person a sport. You have to write three rules for this sport. Do not say what the sport is! Write your three rules in a single forum post. Remember the language we looked at for football rules to help you.

Post your rules by (*insert deadline*).

Possible list of sports
- basketball
- volleyball
- water polo
- figure skating
- rally car racing
- hockey
- baseball
- wrestling
- boxing
- billiards

3 Once all students have posted their rules, post Task 2 and set a deadline for posting guesses.

▶ Task 2: Interaction 1

Now read the rules for other sports in the forum. Can you guess what the sport is? Choose two different posts and guess the sport!

Look at what other people wrote on your post. Did they guess correctly?

If someone correctly guesses the sport, post the answer and tell them well done!

If someone guesses wrongly, then post another rule to help them guess.

Post your two guesses by *(insert deadline)*.

---

4   Once all the sports have been guessed, or almost guessed, post the list of the sports you assigned and congratulate the group. Post any important language corrections at this point if you see them. If you want to extend the activity, you could post Task 3 below (optional).

▶ Task 3: Interaction 2

In this task you are going to create a new, interesting sport! Follow the instructions below.

Choose four rules from this forum.

Each rule must be from a different sport.

Make a new sport with these four rules.

Give your sport a name.

Post the new sport and its rules at the bottom of this forum.

Read the other new sports. Which ones would you like to play?

3.13 Connections

Outline	Students choose two random famous people and then have to try and find as many links as possible between them.
Level	Intermediate and above (B1–C1)
Learning focus	Present simple, past simple, passive
Time	15 minutes
Preparation	All chat rooms (video or text chat rooms) have a feature which allows participants to send private text messages to each other within the chat room. Make sure you and your students know how to do this.

Procedure

1   Arrange a time and open a chat room with your students. Post Task 1.

Task 1: Stimulus

I am going to nominate two people. Each person thinks of a famous person. Send me the name of the person in a private message. Your famous person can be alive or dead.

(Student 1) and *(Student 2)*, please send me your names. Don't post them publicly!

---

2   Once both students have sent you the names, post Task 2. For this task, imagine the names given were Barack Obama and Jackie Chan. Set a deadline of 30 minutes for posting connections. Tell students they must not cut and paste their facts! (If you want to introduce a competitive element, see Activity 3.5 on page 56.)

Task 2: Interaction

Everyone, here are the two names I was given:

- Barack Obama, the first black President of the United States
- Jackie Chan, martial arts expert and actor.

Now you have to think of ways to connect these people. You can use the internet to help you. How many connections can you make in 10 minutes? Go!

You might find, for example:

- that they have met
- that they were headline news on the same day
- that they live in the same country
- that they have the same colour hair.

---

3   Connections students might make are:

Jackie Chan was invited to a White House dinner.

Obama imitated Jackie Chan kicking open a door.

Jackie Chan blogged about Obama.

They are both in the top four most admired men in the world.

Jackie Chan has shaken hands with Obama.

They both wore white shirts at the White House dinner.

A fake story on Twitter about Jackie's death claimed Obama had paid tribute to him.

As students look for connections between the names, you can give them helpful language (see below) or reformulate difficult sentences that come up.

Both of them ...

... starred in ... (movie)

... come from ...

... lived in ...

4   When students have made as many connections as they can in 10 minutes, congratulate them and end the activity. If they enjoyed it, repeat the activity with two different students submitting names to you.

3.14 **Post a recipe**

Outline	Students post a recipe for a food they enjoy eating or eat at a festival or on special occasions. They then comment on or ask questions about others' recipes. The recipes can be used to make a hard copy or online class recipe book.
Level	Elementary and above (A2–C1)
Learning focus	Imperatives (*boil, fry, add, stir, chop*, etc.), food vocabulary
Time	2–3 days
Preparation	No advance preparation required.

Procedure

1   This stage can be done face-to-face or online. Tell students about a recipe you particularly like or that you eat on special occasions. Ask them to comment on whether they would like it or not or whether they have similar dishes in their own countries. Take the opportunity to highlight the cooking verbs (*take, stir, chop, add, beat, mix, boil, fry, bake, roast, grill*, etc.).

2   Set up a forum and give it a name (e.g. *Post a recipe*). Post Task 1, asking students to post a favourite recipe. Set a deadline for posting recipes.

▶ **Task 1: Stimulus**

What is your favourite recipe? Is it a main course, a snack or a dessert? When do you eat it – every day, less often or only for a festival or special occasion? Who cooks it? Where did your family learn the recipe? Have you got a special memory about the recipe?

Post the recipe and some facts or a story about it by *(insert deadline)*.

Use your own words. Don't cut and paste recipes!

---

3   Post Task 2 asking students to comment on each other's recipes. Set a deadline for posting comments.

▶ **Task 2: Interaction**

Read the recipes. Which ones would you like? Do you want to try cooking any? Do you have similar recipes in your country or family? Are there any recipe stories you like?

Post comments on at least three posts by *(insert deadline)*.

(If there are already three comments on a post, choose another post.)

---

4   When everyone has commented, thank students for their participation and end the activity.

Variation

Ask students to upload a picture of their favourite dish. Other students then ask questions about it.

Task 1: Stimulus

What is your favourite dish? Find a picture and post it in the forum.

Post by *(insert deadline)*.

Task 2: Interaction

Look at the pictures. Which dishes would you like to try?

What would you like to know about the dish? For example, you might want to know:

- if people eat the dish for a festival or at a special time
- what ingredients are in the dish
- how to make it
- where the student learned to make the dish and how
- if there are special memories connected to eating the dish.

Choose five posts and make one question for each. Make five different questions – not the same question five times!

Post questions on at least five posts by *(insert deadline)*.

If there are already five comments on a post, choose another post.

3.15 International proverbs

Outline	The teacher posts a word and students find proverbs from different countries about that word. They post the proverb and other students discuss possible meanings.
Level	Upper intermediate and above (B2–C2)
Learning focus	Proverbs
Time	15 minutes per task over three days
Preparation	Find a number of English proverbs for class discussion.

Procedure

1 This stage can be done face-to-face or online. Discuss some English proverbs with the students, e.g.:

Don't cross your bridges before you come to them.

People in glass houses shouldn't throw stones.

A bird in the hand is worth two in the bush.

It never rains but it pours.

Invite students to say what they think the proverbs mean.

2 Set up a forum and give it a name (e.g. *International proverbs*). Post Task 1 and set a deadline for posting proverbs. This post uses the keyword WORDS, but suggestions for other possibilities are given at the end of this activity.

Task 1: Stimulus

I am going to post a word. Your task is to find proverbs and sayings from different countries about that word.

The word is WORDS.

An example of a proverb:

Beautiful words don't put porridge in the pot. (Botswanan proverb)

You can find many sites with proverbs from different countries by typing 'proverbs from different countries' into a search engine. Many of these sites have a search box. Type WORDS into the search box and you will get all the proverbs on that site which are about words.

Post your proverb or saying by *(insert deadline)*.

---

3 When students have posted their proverbs, post Task 2 and set a deadline for posting explanations.

Task 2: Interaction 1

Now look at the proverbs other people have posted. What do you think they mean? Post an explanation for one proverb, for example:

I think 'beautiful words don't put porridge in the pot' means that you need actions as well as words.

If someone has already posted an explanation, choose a different proverb.

Post your explanation by *(insert deadline)*.

---

4   When explanations are posted, post Task 3 and set a deadline for posting comments.

Task 3: Interaction 2

Look at everyone's explanations. Choose three explanations to comment on, e.g.:

I think you need actions as well as words, but sometimes we can just enjoy words, for example in poems or songs.

Post your comments by *(insert deadline)*.

---

5   At the end of the activity, post a summary of what students explained. Feed back with any comments and thank students for their participation.

Other words that yield several proverbs
- *love*
- *money*
- *friends*
- *anger*
- *happiness*
- *wisdom*
- *caution*
- *trust*
- *luck*
- *misfortune*

3.16 Here's the answer

Outline	The teacher provides a series of dates, place names or people's names and students race to type the correct question that would give that answer. This activity works better in a synchronous environment.
Level	Elementary and above (A2–C1)
Learning focus	Question forms, cities and countries, or other topic areas
Time	25 minutes
Preparation	Choose a category and make a list of names, dates or other facts about it. Each item on the list should have an easily identifiable question to go with it. For example, the category 'famous people' could include Barack Obama with the question *Who was the first black president of the United States?* The category could be anything in general knowledge; the example below uses the category 'cities and countries'.

Procedure

1 Set up a live chat session and invite the students. Explain the rules of the game.

Task 1: Stimulus

In this activity I am going to give you a word or phrase in a category. You have to write a question in English that goes with that word or phrase.

For example, if I write *Mount Everest* you can type the question: *What is the highest mountain in the world?*

The category we are going to use is 'cities and countries'. I will type a word. Everyone type a question. When you have typed the questions, I will correct any errors.

---

2 If you think it is necessary, do an example from the list below first.

3 Type the first word in your list. Wait until everyone has typed a question. Make minor corrections at the end to any grammatically incorrect questions and congratulate them on any correct questions. Note that some 'answers' may have more than one appropriate question! Accept all questions that come up, as long as they make sense and are grammatically correct.

4 Continue with the other words in the list until you have finished them.

5 When you have finished, nominate a student and set Task 2.

Task 2: Interaction

Now think of one other word in the same category. *(Student 1)*, your turn. Type your word. Everyone else type questions for the word.

---

6 Repeat Task 2 above for different students. End the activity by thanking students and giving any feedback on the language produced.

7 At the end of the activity, post a summary of what students explained. Feed back with any comments and thank students for their participation.

Sample list for countries and cities

Here are some example items and questions for the category 'countries and cities'. The suggested questions are in brackets.

1   Canada and Mexico *(What countries are on the borders of the USA?)*
2   Rabat *(What's the capital of Morocco?)*
3   8,848 metres *(How high is Mount Everest?)*
4   Between Miami, Puerto Rico and Bermuda *(Where is the Bermuda Triangle?)*
5   Dubai *(Where is the world's tallest building?)*
6   New Amsterdam *(What was the original name of New York?)*
7   Toronto *(What's the biggest city in Canada? Note it is not the capital!)*
8   The kiwi *(What is the national animal of New Zealand?)*

3.17 Check it out

Outline	The teacher posts a series of unusual facts, one of which is invented. Students race to find out which one is the false fact by checking them all. The first student to find the false fact then posts another three unusual facts.
Level	Elementary and above (A2–C1)
Learning focus	Comparatives, present simple
Time	20 minutes per task over a week
Preparation	Find three unusual facts, of which one at least must be false, e.g.:

1   Prince Charles and Prince William of the UK do not travel on the same plane in case of a plane crash. (true)
2   Forest fires move faster uphill than downhill. (true)
3   The Great Wall of China is the only man-made object you can see from space. (false)

Keep a record of where you found these facts.

Procedure

1   This stage can be done face-to-face or online. Share your three facts with students. Start a new forum and give it a name (e.g. *Check it out*). Post Task 1 and set a deadline for posting replies.

Task 1: Stimulus

Read the following three amazing facts. Are they all true? Check it out. Post a reply saying which fact or facts are untrue. You have until *(insert deadline)* to post your reply.

---

2   When a few students have posted, confirm which of your facts are indeed false. Give more detail from your sources and share these if necessary. Then post Task 2 and set a deadline for posting facts.

Task 2: Interaction

Well done! The first person to guess the incorrect fact(s) was *(name of student)*. Now it's his/her turn! He/She now posts three amazing facts. One, two or three of these facts must be false!

Please post your facts by *(insert deadline)*.

---

3   When the next facts are posted, repeat stage 2. Continue this way until at least four students have posted facts.

4   At the end, thank the students for participating. Collect all the true facts together and correct any language errors. You could then use these to make a quick general knowledge quiz by changing them into questions and give it to the students later on in the course. How many can they remember?

3.18 Behind the headlines

Outline	The teacher posts a number of (cryptic) headlines from current newspapers. Students suggest what the stories were. The teacher then assigns each student one headline. They search, find the articles and post a summary.
Level	Intermediate and above (B1–C1)
Learning focus	Narrative tenses, past passive
Time	2–3 days
Preparation	First, research some current news stories and find some cryptic headlines that do not give away too much about the story. An online search using the search term 'weird news' will list several newspaper sites with a selection of bizarre or intriguing stories. You will need 8–10 headlines.

Procedure

1 Set up a forum and give it a name (e.g. *Behind the headlines*). Post Task 1 with the headlines you have chosen, e.g.:

Cat solves mystery of diamond theft

Dark secret revealed after 50 years

Reunited at last!

Missing sailor found

Set a deadline for posting stories.

Task 1: Stimulus

Here are some news headlines:

(insert headlines)

Choose three and suggest what the story might be. Use your imagination!

Post your suggestions by *(insert deadline)*. Then read three other people's suggestions and leave a comment.

---

2 Assign each student one of the headlines by private message and then post Task 2. Set a deadline for posting summaries of the real stories.

Task 2: Interaction 1

Now find out what the real stories were. Research the real story behind the headline that I have sent you and post a short five-line summary.

Post your summary by *(insert deadline)*.

---

3 Post Task 3, asking students to comment on the difference between their imagined stories and the facts. Set a deadline for posting comments.

Task 3: Interaction 2

Read the real news stories and leave a comment on those that surprised you, e.g.:

Wow – the true story is stranger than the imagined one!

This story is exactly what we thought!

The mystery of the theft was really quite simple!

Post your comments by *(insert deadline)*.

---

4   When everyone has commented, end the activity and thank students for their participation.

3.19 All about rhubarb

Outline	Students contribute to a live conversation about a topic they know nothing about by researching it at the same time they are chatting. This activity works better in a synchronous environment.
Level	Elementary and above (A2–C1)
Learning focus	Expressions for adding new information to a conversation and reacting to new information
Time	25 minutes
Preparation	Choose a topic that your students are unlikely to know much about, although they may have heard about it. This could be a recent film that some may have seen, a city that was in the news but that they are unlikely to have visited, a famous person who died but who might not be known to everyone, an exotic animal, a special kind of dish or food that people do not know much about, etc. The example below uses 'rhubarb'. Research some facts about the topic you choose to use as an example.

Procedure

1   This stage can be done face-to-face or online. Make sure the learners are familiar with expressions for introducing and reacting to new information.

Introducing information

Did you know …

I read somewhere that …

I heard that …

I didn't know this, but …

Someone told me …

Reacting to information

Really?

That's interesting. / That's curious.

How interesting!

I didn't know that. / I knew that!

No way!

Huh.

2   Set a time and open your chat room. Make sure the students have the expressions for introducing and reacting to information nearby: this could be on a paper next to them, or on a document open on their computer. Once you have greeted the students, post Task 1.

Task 1: Stimulus

In this task I'm going to give you a topic. I want you to take turns to tell the others something about this topic.

You probably don't know much about this topic! So you will need to open another browser window and search for something to share with the group while the activity is going on.

I'll give you the topic and then give you three minutes to find something you could say about it. When you are ready, type Ready into the chat box.

The topic is *(rhubarb)*.

---

3   Allow students time to research the topic. If they are lower-level, they can do this in their own language providing they translate what they find into English. When they are ready, post Task 2.

Task 2: Interaction

Now we are going to talk about the topic. Here are the rules:

Only post one fact at a time.

Introduce your fact with one of the phrases we saw.

React to another's person's fact with one of the phrases we learned. Here's an example:

A: *Did you know that rhubarb is the name of a plant?*

B: *How interesting! I heard that people cook with it in England.*

C: *Really? Did you know that it's a vegetable, but in the United States it's officially a fruit?*

A: *Huh. I read somewhere that in China it's used for medicinal purposes.*

And so on.

---

4   Once students have contributed their facts, ask them which one they found the most interesting. The person who submitted that fact can then suggest the next topic for discussion.

5   Continue until everyone has suggested a topic. Finish the activity by giving any language feedback necessary and thank the students for their participation.

4 Creative interaction

4.1 Art monologues

Outline	Students imagine they are the character in a painting and write a short monologue expressing what is on the character's mind.
Level	Upper intermediate and above (B2–C1)
Learning focus	Present simple, *wish*, *would like*, describing feelings
Time	Minimum three days (one to post and two to reply)
Preparation	Find several portraits, either contemporary or from different periods of history, that would lend themselves to students thinking about the personalities and inner thoughts of the subject. These could be by famous artists but should not feature historical figures that students are likely to know.

Procedure

1 Set up a forum and give it a name (e.g. *Art monologues*). Post the portraits you have chosen in the forum and number them.

2 Ask students to choose a picture, or private message each student to secretly assign a picture to each. Ask them to think about the man/woman in the portrait:
Think about the person in the portrait.
Give him/her a name.
Is he/she married? Children? Are they a happy family?
What do they like doing?
Think of three adjectives to describe their character.
What are their ambitions and dreams?
What are their fears?

Students should not post their answers, but thinking about them will help them with the next tasks.

3 When you have given the students enough time to think about their character, post Task 1 and set a deadline for posting their monologues.

Task 1: Stimulus

What is on your character's mind? What are they thinking about at the moment? Write a short monologue and post it by *(insert deadline)*.

Write your monologue in the first person. Begin like this:

I'm thinking about …

---

4 When the monologues are completed, post Task 2 and set a deadline for posting guesses. With a larger group, you may have to assign each student a monologue to guess about. Or you can specify that everyone has to choose a different monologue to ask about and it is 'first-come, first-served', which should encourage them to choose quickly.

Task 2: Interaction 1

Look at others' monologues. Choose one and try to guess which picture it is.

Give a reason for your choice, e.g.:

I think this monologue is by the person in picture … because he / she looks worried / happy / sad / scared about …

Post your guess by *(insert deadline)*.

If someone guesses about your monologue, reply and tell them if they are right or wrong.

---

5 When students have guessed or been told the answer, post Task 3 and set deadlines for posting questions and replies.

Task 3: Interaction 2

When you have guessed correctly, think of three things you would like to ask the character, e.g.:

Tell me more about yourself – where do you live?

Tell me about your family.

Post your questions by *(insert deadline)*.

Reply to any questions about your character. Post your reply by *(insert deadline)*.

---

6 Give any necessary language feedback and end the activity by thanking students for their participation.

4.2 Bowl of cherries

Outline	Students post a picture of a household object, a natural object, a food or a means of transport. They then have to link this to an abstract noun (e.g. life, happiness, jealousy) in a saying or proverb (e.g. *Life is a bowl of cherries.*). They interact to find out why others chose that metaphor.
Level	Intermediate and above (B1–C1)
Learning focus	Writing proverbs
Time	2–3 days
Preparation	Find a number of English proverbs in which something concrete is used as a metaphor for something abstract. See the examples below. Activity 3.15 also uses proverbs and could be done as a follow-up or as preparation for this activity.

Procedure

1   This stage can be done face-to-face or online. Introduce students to a number of proverbs and sayings, e.g.:
Life is a bowl of cherries.
People in glass houses shouldn't throw stones.
Jealousy is the green-eyed monster.
The early bird catches the worm.
Love is a burning flame.

Invite the students to identify which abstract concept is being described in terms of something concrete:
life: cherries
criticism: throwing stones
jealousy: monster
punctuality: early bird
love: flame

Ask them to explain the connection, e.g. *Life is a bowl of cherries – one nice thing after another.*

2   Set up a forum and give it a title (e.g. *Bowl of cherries*). Post Task 1 and set a deadline for posting pictures. If you have a small class you may like to amend Task 1 to say 'each of the following' to give the students more pictures to choose from.

Task 1: Stimulus 1

Find a picture of one of the following: a household object, a natural object, a food or a means of transport. Post these by *(insert deadline)*.

---

3   When all the pictures are up, post Task 2, the list of abstract nouns, and the invitation to students to connect them with their picture in a wise saying. Set a deadline for posting sayings.

Task 2: Stimulus 2

Here is a list of abstract nouns:

life, love, jealousy, youth, happiness, anger, wealth, fame, fear, power, pride, curiosity, wisdom

Choose one and connect it with one of the pictures to make a new proverb, e.g.:

Jealousy has as many skins as an onion.

Fame is an empty eggshell.

Don't post an explanation, but have one ready!

Post your saying by *(insert deadline)*.

---

4   When all proverbs are posted, post Task 3 and set deadlines for posting guesses and replies.

Task 3: Interaction

Choose three sayings and guess the explanation behind them, e.g.:

Did you say *Fame is an empty eggshell* because it looks great from the outside but it is meaningless?

Did you say *Fame is an empty eggshell* because famous people are not necessarily what they seem to be?

If three people have posted about one saying already, choose another saying.

When you have three guesses about your own saying, reply giving your own explanation.

Post your guesses by *(insert deadline)* and reply to the guesses by *(insert deadline)*.

---

5   You can collect the proverbs and make a 'proverb poster' using an online curation tool or for classroom display.

Variation
Life's like that

1   Introduce students to three or four sayings about life, e.g. *Life is like a flower*. An internet search for *Life is like …* will reveal more.

2   Introduce the first half of the sayings, e.g. *Life is like a flower …* and invite students to give their explanations, e.g.:
Life is like a flower – it gets more beautiful as it blossoms.

3   Post Task 1 as above. When students have posted, ask them to choose three pictures and to write a *Life is like …* sentence for each of them. They should have an explanation in mind, but not post it.

4   When sentences are posted, ask students to choose three sentences and to complete them with an explanation, e.g.:
Life is like a tube of toothpaste – there is always a bit left in the tube that you can't squeeze out.

5   When all explanations are posted, ask students to choose the six they like best and to combine
    them to make a short poem, e.g.:

Life is like a flower
It gets more beautiful as it blossoms.
Life is like a tube of toothpaste
There is always a bit left in the tube that you can't squeeze out.

4.3 The Royal Hotel story

Outline	Students take it in turns to write a story together from various points of view.
Level	Upper intermediate and above (B2–C1)
Learning focus	Narrative tenses, hotel and tourism vocabulary, collaborative storytelling
Time	Minimum five days depending on class size
Preparation	Find an image of a hotel to put into the first post.

Procedure

1   Tell students they are going to write a story in which they take it in turns to write part of the story, following on from each other. Set up a forum and give it a name (e.g. *The Royal Hotel story*). Post Task 1 and set a deadline for posting characters. This activity works best in classes of around six. If you have a large class, divide the class into two groups in different forums.

▶ Task 1: Stimulus 1

The Royal Hotel

The Royal Hotel is a 200-year-old institution. Many famous people have visited, and people say it has the best service of any hotel in the world. The hotel is also home to many dark secrets, and some believe that a ghost lives in the basement.

You are all going to write a story about the Royal Hotel together. First, invent your character. You will write the story from that character's point of view.

You can choose any one character that would fit into the Royal Hotel setting. This includes rich hotel guests, maids, cleaners, receptionists, waiters, cooks, security guards, etc.

If one person has chosen a character, this doesn't prevent you from choosing the same character. We can have several guests, or several receptionists. It's up to you what you are, but you should keep the same character throughout the story.

Post your characters by *(insert deadline)*.

---

2   Before students write their story, post the rules for writing the story and check that they understand what they have to do. Post Task 2 and set a deadline for introductions and queries.

> **Task 2: Stimulus 2**
>
> Here are the rules for telling the story:
>
> 1   Write in the third person, and use past tenses, e.g. *Charles woke up and went downstairs for breakfast.*
> 2   You cannot write for another person's character, but you can interact with one another in the story. If you have questions, email me.
> 3   Your first post should introduce your character into the storyline. We don't all have to start in the same place. So, for example, one of you could start as a receptionist who is late for work, another could start as a guest waking up in her room, and so on. You will eventually meet up!
> 4   Please do not post more than once in a row.
>
> Post your introduction to the character by *(insert deadline)*.

3   When students have posted their introductions, check for any language difficulties and answer any queries. Post Task 3 and set a deadline for the completed story.

> **Task 3: Interaction**
>
> Now write your story starting with the introduction you posted.
>
> The story will finish on *(insert deadline)*.

4   You can start the story yourself, and set the tone even more (also providing a model). For every new entry in the story, make sure that students post it as a reply to the original post. In this way the story can read from the top of the forum to the bottom.

5   If the posts get mixed up, collect and copy all the parts of the story so far and start a new thread.

6   Encourage the students to work together on this. They can plan 'scenes' if they like but must do it via email. Alternatively, set up a separate thread for students to talk about the story they are creating.

7   Emphasize that the story does not have to have a perfect ending. It might not have a proper ending. It's more about the journey than the destination.

8   At the end of the activity, ask students how they felt about the story and what parts they liked best. At this stage you could conduct some feedback on any language problems that came up during the story.

4.4 Colours

Outline	Students post an image expressing a certain colour. They ask each other what the image means for them and why they chose that one. Then they use the images and explanations to write a poem according to a pattern.
Level	Beginner and above (A1–C1)
Learning focus	Colours, writing a simple poem, the verb *be*
Time	Minimum two days (one to post and one to reply).
Preparation	No advance preparation required.

Procedure

1   Set up a forum and give it a title (e.g. *Colours*). Post Task 1. Set a deadline for posting images and meanings.

▶ Task 1: Stimulus

Think of these colours: white, red, green, blue, yellow.

What do the colours mean for you? Post a picture for each colour to show that meaning, e.g.:

The colour red can mean danger, it can mean warmth, or it can mean love.

Here are three pictures that show these meanings:

Write the meaning with the picture, e.g. *Red is the colour of danger.*

Post your picture and meaning by *(insert deadline)*.

---

2   When everyone has posted, post Task 2 and set a deadline for posting poems.

⬛ Task 2: Poem

Now look at all the pictures.
Choose a colour and make a poem.
Write lines following these patterns:
(colour) *is a/an* (adjective + noun).
(colour) *is the colour of* (noun).
(colour) *is the colour of* (adjective + noun).

Here are two examples:

Green is a new leaf.	*Red is a lovely rose.*
Green is young grass.	*Red is a Valentine heart.*
Green is the colour of spring.	*Red is the colour of love.*
Green is a shiny apple.	*Red is a burning fire.*
Green is a tall tree.	*Red is the setting sun.*
Green is the colour of growing.	*Red is the colour of warmth.*
Green is a bright parrot.	*Red is a warning sign.*
Green is a tiny frog.	*Red is an angry face.*
Green is the colour of life.	*Red is the colour of danger.*

Post your poem by *(insert deadline)*.

---

3 When the poems have been posted, congratulate the students. You can collect their poems and make a poster or put them on an online notice board.

Variation

Similar activities can be devised using pictures to generate phrases or sentences that can then be combined into a poem or other piece of writing, encouraging creativity at lower levels and with limited language. Here are two suggestions:

1 Give the students an abstract noun, e.g. *happiness*, *fear*, *success*, *friendship*. Students post images of what that word means for them. They look at each other's pictures and select five or six to make a poem using the content of the pictures following a set pattern, e.g.:
Happiness is
watching an old movie
talking with friends
And so on.
But most of all, happiness is …

2 Give the students a situation, e.g. *A perfect day out* or *A great holiday,* and ask them to post pictures. Students choose the images they like best and write a 'recipe', e.g.:
A Perfect day out
Take …
Add …
Mix together
And serve with …

4.5 Design a festival

Outline	Students work in groups to design a festival for a particular season, then comment on and ask questions about each other's festivals.
Level	Intermediate and above (B1–C1)
Learning focus	Asking and answering questions, collaborating to design a festival
Time	2–3 days
Preparation	No advance preparation required.

Procedure

1   You could use Activity 3.4: *Find a festival* to prepare for this activity, or simply precede it with a discussion about festivals in different countries (if you have a multicultural class) or about favourite festivals and different family traditions at festivals (if you have a monocultural class).

2   Set up a forum and give it a title (e.g. *Design a festival*). Put students in four groups and create a private message group for each group. Assign each group a season of the year. Their job is to work together to design a festival for that season, then to post a description of the festival. Set a deadline for posting pictures and descriptions.

▶ Task 1: Interaction 1

Invent a festival!
For this task, you are in four groups:
Group 1: Spring
Group 2: Summer
Group 3: Autumn
Group 4: Winter

Work together in your private chat group and invent a festival to celebrate that season. Think about the following questions:

What date is the festival? What does it celebrate?

What food do people eat?

What do people wear?

What do people do (e.g. dance, have a procession, have fireworks, give presents)?

Find a picture to accompany your description (e.g. food, dancing, fireworks) or of the season. Post this in the main forum with a description of the festival.

Post your description of the festival by *(insert deadline).*

---

3   When each festival is posted, post Task 2, inviting students to comment and ask questions about the festivals. Set a deadline for posting comments/questions.

▶ Task 2: Interaction 2

Read about the four festivals on the main forum. Which would you enjoy most? Have you any questions about the festival?

Post your comments or questions by *(insert deadline)*.

---

4   Create a short post summarizing the festivals described (dates and brief descriptions). If you have a course calendar, you could even add the festivals to the calendar and remind students about them each time one comes up!

4.6 **Extreme ironing**

Outline	Students find an 'extreme ironing' photo and post it together with a paragraph from an imaginary blog. They then ask questions and comment on each other's extreme ironing stunts.
Level	Elementary and above (A2–C1)
Learning focus	Narrative tenses, writing a blog
Time	2–3 days
Preparation	No advance preparation required.

Procedure

1   This stage can be done face-to-face or online. Show students this picture and definition and ask for reactions.

'Extreme ironing' is an outdoor activity that combines the danger and excitement of an extreme sport with the satisfaction of a well-pressed shirt.

From *Interaction Online* © Cambridge University Press 2017   PHOTOCOPIABLE

Ask students to imagine they were one of the mountaineering ironing team. Ask them:
Why did you do this?
How did you organize this activity?
Who was with you?

What did friends and family think?
How did you feel when you started climbing up the mountain?
Was it difficult to manage the board and iron as well as climbing up the mountain?
How long did it take you to climb the mountain?
What did it feel like when you got to the top?
What was the descent like?

2   Set up a forum and give it a title (e.g. *Extreme ironing*). Post Task 1 and set a deadline for posting pictures and blogs. Again, students should imagine that they are the people in the picture and write a paragraph describing the event.

Task 1: Stimulus

Extreme ironing isn't always combined with mountaineering. Find a picture of extreme ironing in another situation and post it. Underneath write your 'blog' of the event: a paragraph describing what happened and how you felt.

Use these questions to help you:

Where and when was this picture taken?

Why did you do this?

How did you organize this activity?

Who was with you?

What did friends and family think?

How did you get there?

Was it difficult?

How did you feel?

Post your photo and 'blog' by *(insert deadline)*.

---

3   When the 'blogs' are up, post Task 2 and set a deadline for posting questions.

Task 2: Interaction

Look at other people's photos and blogs. Choose three to ask questions about.
If three people have already asked questions about a post, choose another post.

Post your questions by *(insert deadline)*. Answer any questions about your blog.

---

4   Collect the blogs and photos. Give students feedback and correct errors if necessary. Then make a poster or online pin board.

5   You could follow this up by asking students to choose another student's picture and blog and write a newspaper article about the event. Alternatively, you could ask them to imagine another sport which combines a household chore with a sport.

4.7 Haiku summary

Outline	The teacher posts the plot of a famous book or film as a haiku. Students guess what it is, then post their own.
Level	Intermediate and above (B1–C1)
Learning focus	Summarizing, writing a haiku
Time	2–3 days
Preparation	No advance preparation required.

Procedure

1   This stage can be done face-to-face or online. Discuss the following questions with students:
What are your favourite books or films?
What have you read or watched recently?

2   Set up a forum and give it a title (e.g. *Haiku summary*). If students do not know, explain what a haiku is (a very short Japanese poem with three lines: the first line has five syllables, the second seven and the third five). Explain that in this task they will be writing a haiku, but they should not worry too much about the number of syllables as long as the form is short line – longer line – short line. Post Task 1 with a very short deadline for posting answers.

▶ Task 1: Stimulus

Here are some summaries of films and books in haiku form. Can you guess which books/films they are?

1   *Precious ring is lost.*
Small men with hairy feet
Try to find it.
(Book and film)

2   *Orphan boy*
Buys a broomstick and an owl
Defeats evil lord.
(Book and film)

3   *Old lady tells story*
Of love, ships and icebergs
Lover dies, she survives.
(Film)

Post answers by *(insert deadline)*.

Answers:

1   Lord of the Rings
2   Harry Potter
3   Titanic

3   When the deadline is reached and answers are posted, post Task 2 and set a deadline for students to post their haiku.

▶ **Task 2: Haiku**

Now it's your turn! Choose a film or book that you think your classmates will have read and summarize the plot in a three-line haiku with the following pattern:

Short line

Long line

Short line

Post your haiku by *(insert deadline)*.

Then you will work in teams. Wait for Task 3!

---

4   When the deadline is reached and students have posted their haiku, divide students into two or more teams and assign each team a private message or chat room. Then post Task 3.

▶ **Task 3: Interaction**

Now work in your teams and discuss the haiku. How many can you guess? Try to be the first team to post answers!

---

5   After students have guessed the haiku, post a quick thank you and congratulate the winning team, if there is one.

4.8 Madeleine moments

Outline	Students think of a taste or a smell which conjures up a memory. They write a short passage describing the memory, then choose one post to ask questions about.
Level	Upper intermediate and above (B2–C1)
Learning focus	Narrative tenses, historic present, sense verbs, emotions, writing about memories
Time	2–3 days
Preparation	Make copies of the Proust summary (optional).

Procedure

1 This optional stage can be done face-to-face or online. If you think your students will like it, introduce the students to the famous passage from Proust's novel *Remembrance of Things Past* about eating a madeleine. A simplified and abridged version is given below.

🖱 Task 1: Stimulus 1

One day in winter, as I came home, my mother, seeing that I was cold, offered me some tea. She sent out for one of those little cakes called 'petites madeleines,' and soon I raised to my lips a spoonful of the tea with a piece of the cake. As the warm liquid, and the cake with it, entered my mouth, I suddenly felt a great happiness. Where did it come from? What did it mean?

And suddenly the memory returns. The taste was that of the little piece of madeleine which on Sunday mornings, my aunt Léonie used to give me, dipping it first in her own cup of tea … And once I had remembered the taste, immediately the old grey house where she lived rose up in my mind like the scenery of a theatre, and then I saw the town, the square where I was sent to play before lunch, the streets where I used to walk, the country roads we took when it was fine. In that moment all the flowers in our garden and the water-lilies on the river and the people of the town and their little houses and the church and the whole of the town sprang into being, all from my cup of tea.

From *Interaction Online* © Cambridge University Press 2017   PHOTOCOPIABLE

---

2 Set up a forum and give it a title (e.g. *Madeleine moments*). Post Task 2 and set a deadline for posting memories.

🖱 Task 2: Stimulus 2

Think of one of the following:
- a taste (e.g. a cake your mother baked, a vegetable you hated but had to eat)
- a smell (e.g. mown grass, fresh baking, bonfires).

The taste or smell should conjure up a memory. Write a short paragraph describing your memory. Here are some useful phrases for this task:

The smell/taste of … always reminds me of …

When I smell/taste … it takes me back to a time when …

The first time I smelled/tasted … I was …

Post your memory by *(insert deadline)*.

---

3 When everyone has posted their memories, post Task 3. Set deadlines for posting comments and replies.

▶ Task 3: Interaction

Read everyone's memories. Choose three and leave a question or a comment, e.g.:

Your memory reminded me how much I hated spinach too when I was a child! I like it now though – do you still hate it?

If a memory already has three comments, choose another to comment on.

Post your comments by *(insert deadline)* then reply to any questions about your own post. Reply by *(insert deadline)*.

---

4 Post a summary of the smells and tastes that students mentioned and congratulate them on completing the task.

4.9 Number plate story

Outline	Students discuss personalized number plates. They write up one scenario as a story. They then read each other's stories and comment with alternative scenarios.
Level	Intermediate and above (B1–C1)
Learning focus	Narrative tenses, time expressions, inventing stories about number plates
Time	Minimum two days (one to post and one to reply)
Preparation	Find a picture of a personalized number plate. See example below.

Procedure

1 This stage can be done face-to-face or online. Show students your picture of a number plate or post it online. Ask them:
What is the owner saying about him/herself? How old do you think he/she is?
Would you spend money on a personalized number? Why / Why not?
If you did, what would your number plate say (in six letters)?

2 Set up a forum and give it a title (e.g. *Number plate story*). Post Task 1. Set a deadline of 24 hours for students to decode the plates.

▶ Task 1: Stimulus 1

The following are real number plates from English-speaking countries. What do you think they mean?
SWNDLE
IDIDIT
IM 4 HIM
NOTOLD
I AM L8
YBESLO
BBIOU2
WAS HIS
DTRMND
I MI55 U
OUTAWRK

Post your answers by *(insert deadline)*.

---

3   Post Task 2 with the answers. Let students ask questions about the answers if they have any, and explain some of the conventions (4 = *for*, 8 = *ate*, 2 = *too*, Y = why, BB = baby, U = you, outa = out of).

▶ Task 2: Stimulus 2

Here are the answers:
SWINDLE
I DID IT
I'M FOR HIM
NOT OLD
I AM LATE
WHY BE SLOW?
BABY, I OWE YOU TOO
WAS HIS
DETERMINED
I MISS YOU
OUT OF WORK

Are there any number plates you still don't understand?

---

4   Post Task 3 with an example story and ask students to write their own stories. Set a deadline for posting stories.

▶ Task 3: Story

Now read this story about a number plate.

1 XTREME
Mario was a street performer in New York City. Every day he stood in the square and did a mime of a man who was imprisoned in a box. If the sun shone he went to the square and if it rained he went to the square too, even though people did not give him much money on rainy days. He could not afford to take a day off. He was very poor and lived alone in one room. One day a man in an expensive coat stopped to watch him. He watched for a long time, then took some photos and left. The next day he came back and spoke to Mario. He said he worked for a film company and they needed a mime artist for their next film. He offered Mario the job. The next day they flew to California and started work on the film. Mario saved all his money, thinking he would have to go back to performing on the streets. But to his surprise, the director offered him a big part in his next film. Now Mario is a successful film star and lives in a big house in Beverley Hills with his wife and four children. But Mario never forgets his life on the streets of New York and how lucky he was to escape. That is why he has a number plate that reminds him he has gone from one extreme to the other.

Choose a number plate that you think is interesting. What do you think is the story behind the number plate? Who is the car owner? Why did he/she create that number plate? What happened in his/her life? Write a short, one-paragraph story telling the story behind the plate.

Post your story by *(insert deadline)*.

---

5 Post Task 4. Set a deadline for posting comments on each other's stories.

⬛ Task 4: Interaction

Read your classmates' stories. Choose one and post an alternative explanation.

Post your comments by *(insert deadline)*.

---

6 When all stories are in, you could display them digitally (e.g. online using an online curation tool).

4.10 Dream on

Outline	Students create a dream story using images, then analyse each other's dreams.
Level	Intermediate and above (B1–C1)
Learning focus	Narrative tenses, storytelling
Time	A week for the story, a week for the analysis
Preparation	Find a dream-like picture to post in your forum.

Procedure

1 Set up a forum for this task and give it a name (e.g. *Dream on*).

2 Post the question *What are typical dream images?* Give the following examples and ask students to suggest others:
falling
water
school
a baby
food
being chased
flying

3 Post Task 1. Post your dream-like picture to start, as a stimulus and example for the students. Set a deadline for posting pictures.

Task 1: Stimulus

Here is a picture of something you might see in a dream.

(insert picture)

Now post your own image of something you might see in a dream. You can use the ideas we talked about in this discussion, or your own idea. Please post your dream picture by *(insert deadline)*.

---

4 Once all students have posted their images, post Task 2. Set a deadline for posting stories.

Task 2: Story

Now choose four or five of the pictures you and your colleagues have posted. Create a dream story. Your story must include these pictures, which can be in any order. Please write at least one sentence per picture. You can begin like this:

Last night I had the strangest dream …

Please post your stories by *(insert deadline)*.

---

5 Once all stories are written, post a list of the students' names and post Task 3. Set a deadline for posting replies.

Task 3: Interaction

Find your name on the list. Then look at the name AFTER your name. This is your partner (if your name is the last person on the list, then your partner is the first person on the list).

Find your partner's dream story. Read it again, then write a reply to their story. Tell them what you think the dream means. Use these phrases to help you.

The picture of the … could mean …

You dreamt that you were… This means that you are …

I think the … represents …

Post your replies by *(insert deadline).*

---

6 At the end of the activity, ask students to reply to the dream analysis which their partner wrote. Use the following questions to discuss and complete the task.

Do you think it was a good analysis?

Do you think dreams have real meanings?

What was your favourite dream story here? Do you dream often? Do you remember your dreams?

Variation

For Task 1, you could ask students to find random pictures on the internet. There are several sites that do this. Ask them to use the search term 'random image generator' in a web search. They then select the first random image they like for the activity. You may wish to advise students to be careful with the images they select as a random generator may produce results that are unsuitable for classroom discussion. Alternatively, there are several sites that filter the images so that they are suitable for all ages, so you may prefer to pre-select the site that students use.

4.11 Estate agents

Outline	Students post three pictures of houses with a description of the house. They ask and answer questions about each other's houses, then try to buy the one they like best.
Level	Elementary and above (A2–C1)
Learning focus	House and home vocabulary, answering and asking questions about houses
Time	Minimum three days (one to post, one to question and one to reply)
Preparation	Find some estate agents' details of a number of interesting and varied houses. Look for sample ads using the search terms 'real estate', 'houses for sale', 'estate agents' or 'buy a home'.

Procedure

1   This stage can be done face-to-face or online. Read some estate agents' details with students or post them online and ask students to find the adjectives and phrases designed to sell the house.

2   Set up a forum and give it a title (e.g. *Estate agents*). Post Task 1 and set a deadline for posting adverts. Some students may simply cut and paste the description from the website. You can specify that they need to write their own, or you can decide to let them do this as the real language production comes in the next stage.

Task 1: Stimulus

Look at online pictures of houses. Choose three very different ones to post. Write a short estate agent's description for each, using these questions to help you:

Where is the house? What is it like?

What kind of people is the house good for? (large family / young couple, etc.).

What are the downstairs rooms? What are the upstairs rooms?

Is there a garden?

How much is it?

Remember you want to sell the house, so be very enthusiastic!

Post your advert by *(insert deadline)*.

---

3   After the deadline is up, post Task 2 and set a deadline for posting questions.

Task 2: Interaction

Look at the pictures and descriptions of houses and choose three that you are interested in and want to buy. Ask one question about each house, e.g.:

How big is the garden?

Are the kitchen appliances included?

Post your questions by *(insert deadline)*, then look at your own house pictures and answer any queries as they come in.

---

4   When all questions have been answered, post Task 3 and set a deadline for posting and agreeing a sale.

Task 3: Competition!

Now choose the house you are most interested in buying.

Buyers: Try and bargain for a cheaper price: mention disadvantages (e.g. *The kitchen is very small.*).

Sellers: Try to get the best price: mention the good points about the house (e.g. *The bathroom was recently refitted.*).

You must agree a sale by *(insert deadline)*.

The winner is the estate agent who sells most houses.

---

5   At the end of the activity, thank the students and congratulate them all on any sales they made.

4.12 Make a meme

Outline	Students are given examples of memes and a series of pictures. They choose one and create a meme using an online meme generator.
Level	Elementary and above (A2–C1)
Learning focus	Writing a meme
Time	2–3 days
Preparation	Find examples of meme pictures using the search term 'meme generator'. Look carefully before selecting as some of these sites may contain pictures or messages that are not suitable for classroom use. Select four or five pictures yourself for the first part of the task.

Procedure

1 This stage can be done face-to-face or online. Explain the meaning of the word *meme* (an idea, image, video, etc. that is spread very quickly on the internet) and show students the examples you have selected. Ask them if they have favourite memes they have seen. If necessary, show students how to use a meme generator.

2 Set up a forum and give it a title (e.g. *Make a meme*). Post Task 1 with the pictures you chose. You can if you like, specify a theme for the memes, e.g. childhood, work, food, social media, relationships, science, housework. The example below shows pictures with the theme of animals. Set a deadline for posting captions.

Task 1: Stimulus

Choose one of the following pictures and write a caption for it. Then use a meme generator to make a meme.

Post your meme by *(insert deadline)*.

3   When the memes are all posted, post Task 2 and set a deadline for posting comments.

Task 2: Interaction

Look at everyone's memes. Choose one to comment on.

Post your comments by *(insert deadline)*.

4   You can add a further stage by adding the following sentence to Task 2: *Then post a picture for others to make a meme.*

5   You can follow up this activity by collecting the memes and printing out for a class display or booklet, or creating a board for them using an online curation tool.

4.13 One-way trip to Mars

Outline	Students respond to a series of questions to develop a character on the 'One-way trip to Mars' project, then write imaginary episodes of a reality TV show about the journey arrival, and life on Mars.
Level	Intermediate and above (B1–C1)
Learning focus	Describing people, narrative tenses, space travel, writing scenes for TV
Time	A week
Preparation	The website of the official Mars One project has interesting background information on astronaut selection and the proposed journey. See www.mars-one.com.

Procedure

1 This stage can be done face-to-face or online. Introduce the idea of going on a one-way trip to Mars.

Discuss the following questions with students:
Would you go? The trip is one-way. How would you feel about never coming back?
What kind of people might volunteer?
The expedition is going to be filmed. What problems and difficulties might the volunteers encounter on the journey / when they arrive /with each other?

2 Set up a forum with the title *One-way trip to Mars*. Post Task 1. The questions are designed to help students to develop a character who is going on the journey. Set a deadline for posting pictures and descriptions.

▶ Task 1: Stimulus 1

In this first post you should imagine a character who has volunteered for the Mars expedition. You do not necessarily have to like this character – you could invent someone difficult! Find a picture of what you think this imaginary character might look like and post it, together with a short paragraph based on answers to these questions:

What is your name?
How old are you?
Where are you from?
What languages do you speak?
What's your job?
Are you married? Children?
How fit are you?
Why do you want to sign up for a one-way trip to Mars?
Who are you leaving behind? How do they feel?
Describe your character in five adjectives.
What do you think will be the best things about the trip and life on Mars?
What are some of the problems you might encounter?

Post your picture and answer by *(insert deadline)*.

---

3   Now post Task 2. This is some preparation designed to encourage students to think about their characters and ways they might interact with others. Set a deadline for posting answers.

▶ Task 2: Interaction 1

Read everyone else's character descriptions.
Who do you think your character might get on with?
Is there anyone who might cause difficulties? What kind?

Post your answers by *(insert deadline)*.

---

4   Students are going to collaborate to write a short scene. First, post Task 3 with the rules for writing and check that they understand what they have to do.

▶ Task 3: Stimulus 2

Rules
Together we will write a short scene for a reality TV show.
Here are the rules for writing the script:
1   You can write 'stage directions', e.g.:
    Jo is feeling airsick.
    Or you can write lines that the characters say, e.g.:
    Jo: Oh, I feel so ill …
2   You cannot write for another person's character, but you can interact with one another in the script. If you have questions, email me.
3   Please do not post more than once in a row.

---

5   Now post Task 4. Students write a short scene imagining events as the flight to Mars begins.

Task 4: Interaction 2

The journey begins

The journey to Mars takes about seven months. The astronauts will be together in a confined space. They will be filmed and the film will be sent back to Earth.

Begin with the launch and the first few minutes or so.

What happens? How does your character react?

Work together to write a short scene that will be included in the broadcast on Earth, including events and your character's reaction. The scene begins like this:

Narrator: The launch has been successful and the astronauts are happy and excited. But 20 minutes into the flight, there is a problem…!

Post your lines by *(insert deadline)*.

---

6   When everyone has posted, post Task 5, in which students work together to write a short scene imagining an event five months into the flight.

▶ Task 5: Interaction 3

Almost there

The astronauts have now been together on the flight for five months. It still feels like a long time until they get there!

What happens? Are there any tensions and problems? How does your character react?

Work together to write a short reality TV scene for the TV broadcast, including events and your character's reaction. Begin like this:

Narrator: The astronauts have now been together on the flight for five months. There are another two months to go and they are beginning to feel the stress …

Post your answers by *(insert deadline)*.

---

7   Finally, post Task 6, which takes place once the astronauts have arrived on Mars.

▶ Task 6: Interaction 4

Arrival on Mars

The astronauts have now arrived on Mars.

What happens? Are there any tensions and problems? How does your character react?

Write a short reality TV scene, including events and your character's reaction. Begin like this:

Narrator: Finally the astronauts have arrived on Mars. They are ready to get out of the spaceship and take their first steps on the Red Planet, which will be their home for the rest of their lives …

Post your answers by *(insert deadline)*.

---

8   When everyone has posted, collate the posts and print out to make a display or a booklet or post in online format.

4.14 Fairy tale agony

Outline	Students are given a character from a fairy tale (Cinderella, Rapunzel, etc.). They write a problem page letter asking for advice. Then they post 'agony aunt' replies to each other's letters.
Level	Intermediate and above (B1–C1)
Learning focus	Describing situations and events, narrative tenses, modals for advice and suggestions
Time	Minimum 2–3 days
Preparation	Prepare some background reading/listening or watching of fairy tales for students to refer to. Make a list of two or three suitable sources for students to check.

Procedure

1 This stage can be done face-to-face or online. Private message each student with the name of a fairy tale character. Suitable characters include: Cinderella, Prince Charming, Rapunzel, the Princess from *The Princess and the Pea*, the Princess or the Frog from *The Princess and the Frog*, Snow White, Little Red Riding Hood, Bluebeard's wife, the Little Mermaid, the Ugly Duckling. You can also adapt this activity to involve folk tales or fairy tales from your country, in which case use local fairy tale names.

2 Set up a forum and give it a title (e.g. *Fairy tale agony*). Post Task 1 and set a deadline for posting problems.

Task 1: Stimulus

You have been given the name of a fairy tale character. Read the fairy tale about your character and make a note of your character's problems. The following links will help you:

(insert your links here).

Now write a problem page letter to a magazine (The Fairy Tale Times) explaining your problem. Post this by *(insert deadline).*

Here are some useful phrases for your problem page letter.

Dear Fairy Tale Times,

Let me tell you about my situation …

I'm in terrible trouble …

I have a serious problem …

I don't know what to do about …

---

3 When the deadline is reached, post to the whole group to place students in pairs, e.g.:

Elena, you are partners with Frankie.

Roberto, please work with Xiao Fan.

4   Now post Task 2 to the group, grouping your students in pairs and asking them to reply to each other's problem letters, e.g. *Elena, please reply to Frankie's letter*. Set a deadline for posting replies.

Task 2: Interaction

Please work in the following pairs:

(Student A), please reply to *(Student B's)* letter.

Write a reply to the letter giving advice. You may need to read the appropriate fairy tale before you reply.

Here are some useful phrases for your reply:

Dear …

I'm so sorry to hear about your problem.

If I were you I would …

Here's what I think you should do …

Take my advice and …

You should …

Remember, you don't have to …

Whatever you do, don't …

Post your reply by *(insert deadline)*.

---

5   After everyone has posted, the students can read the letters and replies and comment if they wish. Who had the best problem? What was the best advice?

4.15 Our reporter on the spot

Outline	The teacher posts 6–8 unusual pictures. Students choose one and write a headline. Students choose one headline and picture and interview the author as if they were an eyewitness, then write an article about it.
Level	Intermediate and above (B1–C1)
Learning focus	Narrative tenses, past passives, writing a newspaper article
Time	2–3 days
Preparation	Find 6–8 unusual pictures that each suggest a news story. You could do this by using a random image generator (see Activity 4.10: *Dream on*) or selecting pictures from existing news websites.

Procedure

1 Set up a forum and give it a title (e.g. *Our reporter on the spot*). Post the pictures you have found. Then post Task 1 and set a deadline for posting pictures and headlines.

Task 1: Stimulus

Look at the pictures and select one. Imagine it appears on the front page of a newspaper. Write a headline to accompany the picture. Remember the following points about headlines:

- They are usually short, e.g. *Students protest university fees*
- They are usually in present tense, e.g. *Large storm hits city centre*
- There aren't usually any articles, e.g. *President signs education law*

Post your headline together with the picture you have chosen.

Post your picture and headline by *(insert deadline)*.

---

2 When all headlines are posted, post to the whole group to place students in pairs, e.g.:
Fatima, please work with Maria.
Juan, please work with Xiao Fan.
Try to pair students who have chosen different pictures.
Then post Task 2, and set deadlines for conducting interviews and posting stories.

Task 2: Interaction

Work in your pairs.

1 *(Student A)*, interview *(Student B)* about their news story. *(Student B)*, imagine you were an eye witness of the story.

2 Then *(Student B)*, interview *(Student A)*.

You have till *(insert deadline)* to interview each other.

Then look back at your partner's replies to your questions. Write them as a news story, e.g.:

DRAMATIC FLOODS IN SW ENGLAND!
The recent heavy rain has caused widespread flooding in the south of the country. Many roads are underwater and residents have been evacuated from their homes. We spoke to Mrs Eliot, who was evacuated last night from her home in Burnt Norton.
'It was terrible,' she said, tearfully. 'The downstairs rooms are full of water. I was trapped in an upstairs bedroom.'

Post your story by *(insert deadline)*.

---

3 Let everyone read each other's stories. You can collect them and 'publish' them as a newspaper, either on paper or online.

4.16 Sci-fi sequence

Outline	Each student posts a picture with a science-fiction theme (e.g. rocket, alien planet, space invader). Assign each student a number. Student 1 chooses a picture and posts the beginning of a sci-fi adventure story. Student 2 continues, and so on.
Level	Intermediate and above (B1–C1)
Learning focus	Narrative tenses, place description, adjectives for feelings and sensations, writing a collaborative story
Time	2–3 days
Preparation	Find a short science-fiction story for students to read before they write their own. You can find nice short ones by doing a keyword search for 'flash fiction', 'science fiction' or 'very short science fiction'.

Procedure

1 Set up a forum and give it a name (e.g. *Sci-fi sequence*). Post Task 1 and set a deadline for posting pictures.

Task 1: Stimulus

Find a science-fiction picture online. Here are some ideas for keywords you could search for:

spaceship

UFO

alien planet

space station

alien

extra-terrestrial

Alternatively, choose an image from a science-fiction film or TV show you like.

Post your picture in this forum. Please post it by *(insert deadline)*.

---

2 When all the images are posted, assign each student a number, then post Task 2 and set a deadline for completing the story.

Task 2: Interaction

You are going to write a science-fiction story together, using these pictures.

Student 1 begins. Choose a picture and write the beginning of the story.

Then it is Student 2's turn. Choose another picture and describe what happens next.

Continue like this. Student *(insert final student number)* is the last student. You will have to end the story!

Complete your story by *(insert deadline)*.

---

3   At the end, collect all the posts and put them together so they form one large story. For homework, students could write a short summary of the story.

Variation
You can use other genres for the stimulus (e.g. western, adventure movie, police show). For the interaction and final product, change the story to a video game, a television series, a plot for a movie, etc.

4.17 This will change your life

Outline	The teacher posts a list of categories for adverts, e.g. cleaning products, health supplements. Students pick one, source a picture and write an advert. They read each other's adverts and write *A satisfied customer comments* or *An unhappy customer complains*.
Level	Intermediate and above (B1–C1)
Learning focus	Imperatives, superlatives, will for promises, question forms, present simple, adjectives for emotions, writing an advert for a product
Time	2–3 days
Preparation	Find some examples of persuasive adverts.

Procedure

1 This stage can be done face-to-face or online. Share some examples of persuasive adverts with the students. Draw their attention to features commonly found in adverts, such as:

- superlatives (e.g. *The best soap powder you will ever use!*)
- rhetorical questions (e.g. *Is housework getting you down?*)
- promises (e.g. *This will change your life!*)
- imperatives (e.g. *Buy one today!*).

2 Set up a forum and give it a title (e.g. *This will change your life*). Post Task 1. Set a deadline for posting pictures and adverts.

Task 1: Stimulus

Here are some categories for products:
- Beauty products
- Health supplements
- Cleaning products
- Convenience foods
- Household gadgets
- Cars.

Choose one category. Find a picture of a product and write an advert for it. Try to convince people to buy it! Say what it will do for them and how it will improve their lives.

Post your picture and advert by *(insert deadline)*.

---

3 When everyone has posted, post Task 2 and set a deadline for posting comments.

Task 2: Interaction

Read the adverts. Now imagine you have bought three of the products. Decide whether you are very happy or very unhappy with them. Leave a comment with the heading *A satisfied customer comments* or *An unhappy customer complains*, e.g.:

A satisfied customer comments: *I am delighted with your new skin cream Lift! I have used it once and already look years younger!*

OR

An unhappy customer complains: *I am very unhappy with your cleaning product Shine! I used it once and it left stains all over my walls.*

If an advert already has three comments, choose a different advert.

Post your comments by *(insert deadline)*.

---

4   Once students have posted their adverts, post a quick summary naming the products and adverts. Give language feedback as usual and thank the students for their adverts.

Variation

This activity could be used as a follow-up to Activity 4.19: *Crazy machines*. Write an advert to market your invention and give customer feedback.

4.18 Thirteen ways of looking

Outline	Students read the poem *Thirteen Ways of Looking at a Blackbird* by Wallace Stevens. The teacher posts a picture of an object and messages each student with another word which can trigger a mental image about the object. Students work together to create their own version of the poem about the object.
Level	Intermediate and above (B1–C1)
Learning focus	Present simple, describing objects, writing a collaborative poem
Time	2–3 days
Preparation	Find the poem *Thirteen Ways of Looking at a Blackbird* by Wallace Stevens. You can find this poem online by doing a search for the title and the author. Then find a picture of an object that students will use to write their own poem. The example below is based on a violin.

Procedure

1 This stage can be done face-to-face or online. Ask students to find the poem *Thirteen Ways of Looking at a Blackbird* by Wallace Stevens. Read the poem with them. Verses VII, VIII, X, and XI are more difficult than the others, so if you think they are too difficult for your group, you could omit them and present an abridged poem: *Nine ways of Looking at a Blackbird*. Prepare as many evocative words or phrases about the picture you are going to use as there are students in your group. For example, here are some words and phrases for the image of a violin:

polished wood	*face*
concentration	*fingers*
dancing	*orchestra*
harmony	*solo*
melody	*dancing*
notes	*rhythm*
bow	

2 Set up a forum and give it a title (e.g. *Thirteen ways of looking*). Post the picture of your object with Task 1. Private message each student with one of the evocative words. Set a deadline for posting verses.

Task 1: Stimulus

Look at the picture of the violin. Together we are going to write a poem called *(number of students in group) Ways of Looking at a Violin*. Everyone will write one short verse. I will message you with a word. You must use the word in your verse about the violin. For example, if your word is *strings*, you might write something like:

The violinist tightens the strings.

They are ready for the bow.

Your verse should be 2–4 lines long. It should paint a picture of the object. Think of your reader: they should be able to see the 'picture' in their minds.

Post your verse by *(insert deadline)*.

---

3   Task 2 involves each of the students selecting from the verses to create a poem. This means that the total number of verses will be greater than the number of verses you specify, so for example, if you have 20 students in your class, you could specify that the poem is called *Eleven Ways of Looking at a Violin*.

Decide on the number of verses you want the poem to have and post Task 2. Set a deadline for posting complete poems.

Task 2: Poem

Now you are going to put the verses together to make a poem. Choose *(insert number)* of the verses and decide on the best order. Copy and paste them to make a poem and post your poem.
Post by *(insert deadline)*.

---

4   When all the poems have been posted to the forum, post Task 3 and set a deadline for posting comments.

Task 3: Interaction

Read the poems and comment on them. Say what you like about them, for example:

Cristina, your poem gave me a really vivid picture of gypsies dancing!

Megumi, your poem made me think about how all the different notes from all the different instruments in the orchestra come together to make a melody.

Post by *(insert deadline)*.

---

5   When everyone has commented, thank students for their participation and end the activity.

Variation
Instead of all using one picture, assign each student a different evocative word or picture by private message. They all begin writing the first verse of the poem. Then each person visits a different student's poem and writes another verse there. Continue this way until everyone has written a verse on everyone else's poems.

Suggested words that work with this activity: *mountain, pen, pencil, horse, leaf, handbag, book, door, tower.*

4.19 Crazy machines

Outline	Students look at Rube Goldberg's crazy machines. They choose one and post a description of how it works. Then they design their own machine for a simple task. Students comment on each other's machines and choose the three they would find most useful, giving reasons.
Level	Upper intermediate and above (B2–C1)
Learning focus	present simple, *when* ... , present passive, relative clauses
Time	2–3 days
Preparation	Find a copy of Rube Goldberg's Self-Operating Napkin online using the search term 'self-operating napkin'.

Procedure

1 Set up a forum and give it a name (e.g. *Crazy machines*). Introduce the students to the Self-Operating Napkin. Show the illustration in class or post it.

Self-Operating Napkin

Ask them to discuss how the machine works. They can do this in pairs in class or post explanations if online. Then give them or post the explanation:

When the diner takes a mouthful of soup (A), the spoon pulls the string (B). The string raises the ladle (C), which throws a biscuit (D) up to the parrot (E). The parrot jumps off his perch to catch the biscuit. His perch (F) tilts, and a weight (G) falls into the bucket (H). The weight in the bucket pulls a string (I), which lights a cigarette lighter (J). This sets off a firework (K). The firework is attached to a sickle (L). When the firework goes off, the sickle (L) cuts a string (M) which is attached to a pendulum. When the string is cut, the pendulum can swing and the napkin wipes the diner's chin.

Then brainstorm a list of everyday tasks with the students (e.g. getting out of bed, getting dressed, laying the table, eating spaghetti, eating hot soup).

2   Post Task 1 and set a deadline for posting pictures and descriptions.

Task 1: Stimulus

Use a search engine to find examples of Rube Goldberg's famous machines using the search terms 'Rube + Goldberg + inventions'.

Choose one you like and share it with the group. Post two or three sentences about how it works. You can use the text about the Self-Operating Napkin to help you.

Post your favourite machine by *(insert deadline)*.

3   When all descriptions are posted, post Task 2 and set a deadline for posting pictures and explanations.

Task 2: Invention

Look at the list of everyday tasks we brainstormed earlier and choose one. Now design a machine to help do that task. Draw your machine and write a short explanation of it. Upload the drawing and explanation to our forum by *(insert deadline)*.

4   When the drawings and explanations are posted, post Task 3 and set a deadline for posting comments.

Task 3: Interaction

Look at everyone's inventions. Make comments on at least three other inventions. Reply to any comments or questions about your invention.

Post your comments by *(insert deadline)*.

5   When students have finished commenting, ask everyone to choose the invention they would find most helpful and say why.

5 Critical interaction

5.1 Balloon debate

Outline	Students are passengers in a hot air balloon which is too heavy and have to decide which of the others in the group most deserves to stay.
Level	Intermediate and above (B1–C1)
Learning focus	Language of hypothesis and recommendation: *should*, *would*
Time	10–15 minutes for Task 1, 15–30 minutes for Task 2 over three days
Preparation	No advance preparation required.

Procedure

1. If you have more than six students in the group, put them in pairs for each of the role cards. Set up a forum and give it a title (e.g. *Balloon debate*). Post Task 1 and send each student or pair of students a role (see suggested roles on page 129, although you may prefer to make up your own). Set a deadline for posting introductions.

> **▶ Task 1: Stimulus**
>
> You are all travellers on a hot air balloon across the mountains. Read your role card, and then introduce yourself to the group.
>
> Post your introduction by *(insert deadline)*.

2. When everyone has posted, post Task 2 and set a deadline for posting opinions.

> **▶ Task 2: Interaction**
>
> Now read about all the other travellers in the balloon. There is a problem. The balloon is going down because the load is too heavy. One person has to jump out of the balloon to save the rest. Who should stay? Discuss who you think is the most important person to keep on the balloon. You can choose anybody BUT NOT YOURSELF.
>
> You can comment on other people's posts and try to convince them.
>
> Post your opinions by *(insert deadline)*.

3. When the deadline has been reached, ask students to vote formally for the person they think should stay (if they haven't already). They post the name of the person in the forum. The person with the fewest votes has to jump! If there is a tie for the smallest number of votes then repeat the vote with only those people eligible to be voted for.

Variation

You can use this format for other similar discussions, e.g.:

Who deserves the scholarship?
Who gets the heart transplant?
Who should get a pardon for his/her crimes?
Who should represent the country at an important event?

You will need to adapt the role cards for any of these variations. Alternatively, let students create their own.

Role cards for Balloon debate

 Role card 1

You are a 24-year-old Olympic athlete. You have spent most of your life doing sports for your country and have won many medals, but you are intending to represent your country at the next Games.

 Role card 2

You are a 60-year-old scientist. You are working on a cure for cancer and you believe you are very very close to discovering it. You only need a couple more years.

 Role card 3

You are a single mother of three small children. The children's father died a year ago so you are the only person who can provide for your children. You are 32 years old.

 **Role card 4**

You are the newly elected president of the country. You won the majority of the votes and everyone says you are the best hope the country has had in over 30 years. You are 55 years old.

 Role card 5

You are the 29-year-old star of the most successful television show in the country. You are very well known and popular across all age and interest groups.

 Role card 6

You are a very rich owner of a big company. You are 70 years old. You have just remarried and are desperate for some extra years of life to enjoy with your new young spouse. You have the most money of the people in the balloon and will pay a lot to stay alive.

From *Interaction Online* © Cambridge University Press 2017   PHOTOCOPIABLE

5.2 **We see things differently**

Outline	Students are all shown the same picture but have to describe it in different ways according to roles they are assigned.
Level	Intermediate and above (B1–C1)
Learning focus	Adjectives, descriptive language
Time	10 minutes per task over two days
Preparation	Find a picture of a place to live that students could react to from different perspectives (e.g. small town, big town, skyscraper, old-fashioned house, hot place, cold place). The activity uses the example of a small village.

Procedure

1   Open a forum thread and give it a name (e.g. *We see things differently*). Post your picture and the instructions for Task 1. Set a deadline for posting descriptions.

Task 1: Stimulus

Look at this picture. Take turns and write sentences describing it. Describe what you see.

Post your descriptions by *(insert deadline)*.

---

2   Allow students to build up a description of the picture together. Once everyone has posted something, divide the class into two groups and post Task 2. Set a deadline for posting comments.

Task 2: Interaction

Now I'm going to divide you into two groups, A and B. Here are the groups:
Group A: *(insert students' names)*
Group B: *(insert students' names)*

Read the role information for your group:
Group A: You live in a small village like this and you HATE it. You think life is boring, everybody knows each other's business and there is nothing to do.

Group B: You live in a big city. Your DREAM is to live in a place like this. You think the quality of life is better, it's better for families and it's just nicer.

Now, look at the picture again. In your role, post one sentence in reaction to this picture. Don't repeat what your information says, just write a sentence about the picture. Students from Group A and Group B should alternate, like this:

A: *I can see a very boring place. Maybe only 100 people live here.*

B: *This looks like a lovely little village.*

A: *There are no shops, no cinema, no clubs in this picture.*

B: *There are lots of green spaces for children to play.*

And so on.

Post your sentences by *(insert deadline)*.

3　Allow students to post their comments. If it helps, assign each student a number to decide on the order of posting.

4　At the end, summarize the posts. Ask students if they can think of other occasions where a person's background might influence the way they see things.

5　If you want to extend this activity, you could use this as a way to expand students' vocabulary by making a table of adjectives with neutral, positive or negative connotations (e.g. *busy, bustling, crowded*).

5.3 Virtual summit

Outline	Students are given roles with different strategies for encouraging public health and fitness. They discuss their positions and then act out their parts in a simulated government panel on initiatives for improving health.
Level	Upper intermediate and above (B2–C1)
Learning focus	Debating language
Time	10–15 minutes for Task 1 and 30–45 minutes for Task 2 over a week
Preparation	Research some government initiatives in various countries for improving health and fitness, by doing a search using the search term 'government initiatives on health and fitness'.

Procedure

1 This stage can be done face-to-face or online. Discuss the government initiatives you researched with students. This will help them generate ideas for the discussion activity that follows.

2 Set up a main forum and give it a title (e.g. *Virtual summit*). Post Task 1 which explains how the activity works.

▶ Task 1: Stimulus

In this forum you are going to role play a virtual summit on public health. Read the following background information:

You are part of a government panel discussing ways of improving health through diet and fitness. They have called together a large group of experts to present ideas on what direction the organization should take.

One of the constraints will be budget. It is expected that improvements in public health will lead to lower medical bills, but each group should show how their ideas will be cost-effective. Each group will present its ideas to a panel of judges.

The judges will have time to ask questions. At the end of the summit, the judges will award the stewardship and budget of the new organization to one of these groups.

---

3 Divide the class into five groups: four groups each to prepare a statement of ideas, and a panel of judges who will decide which idea to adopt. Set up a closed forum for each group. Send each group a role card (see page 134). Post Task 2 and set a deadline for posting statements. While the groups are doing this, the judges can discuss and decide on a title for the campaign.

▶ Task 2: Interaction 1

Read your role card. In your group, work together to prepare a statement outlining your position. Post your group's statement of ideas in the main forum.

Post your statement by *(insert deadline)*.

---

4 Once the statements have all been posted to the forum, post Task 3. The judges' panel may post questions to the different groups. If the judges ask a question about a post, only the group who posted the original may answer.

Set a deadline for posting questions and answers. Once the deadline is reached, the judges post their final decision.

▶ Task 3: Interaction 2

Groups 1–4: the judges may ask you questions about your proposed plans. You can only answer questions about your own group's plans!

All questions should be posted and answered by *(insert deadline)*.

Judges: You can discuss all the plans while the groups are posting! Then decide which group's idea you are going to adopt. Post your decision with reasons by *(insert deadline)*.

---

5 Round off the activity by thanking students for their participation.

Variation
Instead of a health and fitness initiative, you could use one of the following scenarios:
*   deciding on aspects of a community centre (see example and roles on page 135)
*   deciding on an opening ceremony for a sporting event
*   choosing the best form of alternative energy for a new town
*   deciding on a way of getting more people to use public transport.

Role cards for Virtual summit: Health and fitness initiative

Judges

You have been appointed to decide how this new National Health and Fitness initiative will proceed. Several interest groups will present their ideas. You should read their initial presentations and ask questions if you think anything is unclear. At the end of the summit you must decide which group(s) have the best ideas. First, think of a title for the initiative!

Group 1: Healthy meals for kids

You think that supplying free healthy and nutritional meals to schoolchildren is the way to encourage healthy eating habits early on – habits which will last a lifetime! Think up some convincing arguments why this is the best way to use the money in the budget and also how you could offset the cost (e.g. through tax).

You should present your view to the summit by *(insert deadline)*. The judges may ask you questions, which you should answer.

Group 2: Free sports facilities

You think that making facilities such as pools and gyms free of charge would encourage people to become more active. Cities could also provide free bikes and more cycle tracks to encourage people to cycle to work, not drive. Think up some convincing arguments why this is the best way to use the money in the budget and also how you could offset the cost (e.g. through tax).

You should present your view to the summit by *(insert deadline)*. The judges may ask you questions, which you should answer.

Group 3: Advertising campaign

You think that a campaign warning of the dangers of an unhealthy life is the best way to reach the maximum number of people! It could be targeted especially at at-risk groups. Think up some convincing arguments why this is the best way to use the money in the budget and also how you could offset the cost (e.g. through tax).

You should present your view to the summit by *(insert deadline)*. The judges may ask you questions, which you should answer.

Group 4: Health food subsidies

You think that subsidizing healthy food in shops is the best way to encourage people to eat healthily. Healthy food tends to be expensive and junk food is cheap – if this situation were different, more people would eat healthily! Think up some convincing arguments why this is the best way to use the money in the budget and also how you could offset the cost (e.g. through tax).

You should present your view to the summit by *(insert deadline)*. The judges may ask you questions, which you should answer.

Virtual summit: Scenario 2 and variation suggestions

Here is an example with role cards for another scenario. Below are alternative scenarios you could try, developing your own role cards on the models given. The sentences in bold in the example are the only sentences you will need to change when making role cards for a different scenario. The stages of the activity are the same as for the health and fitness initiative on pages 132–3.

 Task 1: Stimulus

In this forum you are going to role play a virtual summit on a new community centre for your area. Read the following background information:

You are part of a government panel discussing ways of bringing communities together through community centres. They have called together a large group of experts to present ideas on what direction the organization should take.

One of the constraints will be budget. Each group should show how their ideas will be cost-effective and contribute to bringing the community together. Each group will present its ideas to a panel of judges. The judges will have time to ask questions. At the end of the summit, the judges will award the stewardship and budget of the new organization to one of these groups.

Role cards for Virtual summit: Community centre

✂ ---

Judges

You have been appointed to decide how a new community centre initiative will proceed. Several interest groups will present their ideas. You should read their initial presentations and ask questions if you think anything is unclear. At the end of the summit you must decide which group(s) have the best ideas. First, think of a title for the initiative!

✂ ---

Group 1: Teenagers and young people's initiative

You think that teenagers and young people in your community don't have enough to do and this has an effect on mental health and crime. Think up some convincing arguments why this is the best way to use the money in the budget and also how you could offset the cost (e.g. through tax).

You should present your view to the summit by *(insert deadline)*. The judges may ask you questions, which you should answer.

✂ ---

Group 2: Senior citizens

You think older people in your community are isolated and lonely. A community centre could provide ways for them to socialize. Think up some convincing arguments why this is the best way to use the money in the budget and also how you could offset the cost (e.g. through tax).

You should present your view to the summit by *(insert deadline)*. The judges may ask you questions, which you should answer.

✂ ---

---✂---

 Group 3: Fitness programmes

You think that a programme of fitness classes could help the community both healthwise and socially. It could be targeted especially at at-risk groups. Think up some convincing arguments why this is the best way to use the money in the budget and also how you could offset the cost (e.g. through tax).

You should present your view to the summit by *(insert deadline)*. The judges may ask you questions, which you should answer.

---✂---

 Group 4: Evening classes

You think that a programme of evening classes in a range of subjects would attract a lot of people. Think up some convincing arguments why this is the best way to use the money in the budget and also how you could offset the cost (e.g. through tax).

You should present your view to the summit by *(insert deadline)*. The judges may ask you questions, which you should answer.

---✂---

5.4 Making improvements

Outline	Students take turns making recommendations to improve an aspect of their town and asking each other about another aspect.
Level	Intermediate and above (B1–C1)
Learning focus	Describing problems (*not enough … too much … too many*) and making recommendations
Time	30 minutes over 3–4 days
Preparation	No advance preparation required.

Procedure

1   Assign each student a number and post the list of names and numbers for the activity. Choose an aspect of town life for which it is easy to think of improvements. The example is based on the students' home town.

2   Set up a forum and give it a title (e.g. *Making improvements*). Post Task 1 and set a deadline for posting suggestions for improvements and questions.

Task 1: Stimulus and Interaction

In this activity we are going to make suggestions about how to improve things in our home town. I'll start by giving an example about public transport:

There is too much traffic and not enough public transport in my town. I think more frequent and more punctual buses and trains would improve life here.

Now, (*Student 1*), it's your turn. What is public transport like in your town? Post two improvements you would like to see. Please post your improvements by (*insert deadline*).

When you have finished, ask (*Student 2*) a question about a different aspect of his/her town. Here are some ideas to help you choose:

- Leisure facilities
- Sports
- Shopping
- Safety
- Parks and natural spaces
- Schools and universities

Please post your reply and next question by (*insert deadline*).

---

3   Students continue like this, answering the last person's question and then posing a new question to the next person.

4   At the end of the activity, summarize (or nominate a student to summarize) all the list of improvements made. Ask students to say which ones have already been implemented in their home towns (if they come from different towns), or which ones they think might eventually happen one day!

5.5 **Mystery puzzle**

Outline	One student is given a mystery puzzle and the other students have to work out the answer by asking questions and thinking laterally.
Level	Intermediate and above (B1–C1)
Learning focus	Past tense, *Yes/No* questions
Time	Two days
Preparation	No advance preparation required.

Procedure

1 Set up a forum and give it a title (e.g. *Mystery puzzle*). Choose a student (Student A) and send them a mystery riddle and the solution. Then post Task 1 and set a deadline for posting solutions to the puzzle. See below for some example mystery riddles and solutions, or you could invent your own riddles.

Task 1: Stimulus and Interaction

I have given *(Student A)* a mystery. He/she is going to share it with you and has the solution. You need to solve the mystery! You can ask questions, and *(Student A)* will answer, but they can only answer YES or NO.

You can only answer one question at a time.

If you think you know the mystery, post the answer. *(Student A)* will tell you if it is correct.

(Student A), please post the mystery. After that you have until *(insert deadline)* to solve it!

---

2 Let the students try and solve the mystery. If they are getting stuck, suggest to the student who holds the mystery that they can give a clue or point the group in the right direction.

3 At the end of the activity, congratulate the group. If you like, the person who solved the mystery could be given another mystery or you could ask them to find one online using the search term 'mystery riddles and answers' to share with the group. Then you can join in!

Sample mystery riddles

1 A man was in a room. A woman entered. She was carrying a closed cardboard box and she sat down near the man. The man couldn't see, hear or smell the box's contents, but he knew what was in the box.
(Solution: The box contained a cat, and the man was allergic to cats and began to get an allergic reaction.)

2 A woman went into a restaurant. She ordered a large meal, and paid nothing for it.
(Solution: The woman was a famous actress. A fan saw her sign a cheque for the meal, and wanted the autograph. So he went to the manager and paid for the meal to get the cheque. The cheque never went to the bank so the woman didn't pay.)

3 There was a green house. Inside the green house there was a white house. Inside the white house there was a red house. Inside the red house there were lots of babies. What is it?
(Solution: a watermelon.)

4 Two girls were at a party. They were drinking iced tea. One girl drank very fast and had finished five in the time it took the other to drink just one glass. The girl who drank one glass died. The other girl who drank five glasses survived. All of the drinks were poisoned. How did the girl who drank the most survive?
(Solution: The poison was in the ice cubes.)

5.6 My take on ...

Outline	Students work in groups to discuss different questions. They post opinions on their questions and then comment on and discuss each other's posts.
Level	Intermediate and above (B1–C1)
Learning focus	Language for giving opinions
Time	20 minutes per task over 3–4 days
Preparation	Choose a topic with a broad appeal to your learners and that has many different possible angles that could be explored. Create a series of questions about this topic. You should have four sets of questions on the topic with 3–4 questions in each set. Useful topics for this kind of activity are:

- the media
- private education
- large sports events (e.g. World Cup, Olympics)
- fashion
- video games
- diets.

Procedure

1 Divide students into groups of three or four and set up a closed group for each (the example has four students in the group). Give each group a name (e.g. *My take on newspapers*). Assign each student a letter A, B, C, or D. Private message all the Student As with one set of questions, all the Student Bs with another set and so on, so that they do not see each other's questions. The example below is based on newspapers. Then post Task 1 in each forum and set a deadline for posting opinions.

▶ Task 1: Stimulus

You each have a different set of questions on the same topic: newspapers. Think about your questions and post your answers to the forum. Post your opinions on the questions you have been given by *(insert deadline)*.

(Student A questions)
1 Do you have both tabloid and serious newspapers in your country? What is the difference? Which do most people read? What effect does this have?
2 Do you think that newspapers report events responsibly?
3 Is truth or profit more important to newspapers? What effect does this have?

(Student B questions)
1 Do you think newspapers should have complete freedom to investigate people's private lives?
2 Do you think there should be any censorship of media, e.g. to protect children?
3 Is there a political bias in the media in your country? Do you think the media should be regulated to stop political bias?

(Student C questions)
1   Who owns the media in your country? What are the issues when several or all newspapers are controlled by one body – person or state?
2   Do you think the media has too much power over people's opinions?
3   Do you think the media has got better or worse over the last 50 years?

(Student D questions)
1   Why do people still buy newspapers when information is available online?
2   Do you trust what you read online?
3   Would you rather have free TV with adverts or pay a licence fee and have no adverts?

2   When everyone has posted their opinions, post Task 2, asking them to comment on each other's opinions. Set a deadline for posting comments.

► Task 2: Interaction 1

Now read each other's posts and comment on them, saying if you agree or disagree and giving reasons. Add any ideas of your own. Post your comments by *(insert deadline)*.

3   When all comments are posted, set up a common forum to include all groups and post Task 3 (optional). Set a deadline for posting summaries.

► Task 3: Interaction 2

Now read everybody's comments about your three questions. Write a short summary of what you all thought, e.g.:

Student C: *In my group we thought that newspapers should not be controlled by the state because they would only give the opinion of the government, but we also thought it was dangerous if many newspapers and TV channels were owned by one person, because then they could force the journalists to give only their opinions.*

Post in this main forum by *(insert deadline)*, then read the summaries and compare what the different groups thought.

4   The summaries could be used as a starting point for students to write an essay on the media, if appropriate for your class.

5.7 Multiple devil's advocate

Outline	Students take turns playing devil's advocate based on the topic of online piracy.
Level	Intermediate and above (B1–C1)
Learning focus	Agreeing and disagreeing, linkers to show contrast (*however, on the other hand ...*)
Time	10–15 minutes per task over five days
Preparation	Choose a topic that could be easily debated by your students and form a statement about it, similar to a motion in a debate. Possible statements:

- All testing on animals should be banned.
- Single-sex schools are good for education.
- The internet should be censored.
- Advertising hurts people.
- Movie or music piracy is not a serious crime.

The example below is based on the last statement and topic of piracy. Find a video about your topic (in this case online piracy using the search terms 'online piracy', or 'online piracy pros and cons') to share with students.

Procedure

1   Set up a forum and give it a title (e.g. *Multiple devil's advocate*). Post Task 1 and set a deadline for posting comments. Post a brief comment yourself on this statement to give the students a model.

▶ Task 1: Stimulus

Look at the following statement:

Movie or music piracy online, if done by individuals, is not a serious crime.

Think about the video you saw, and your own feelings about this statement. Do you agree or disagree? Leave a very brief comment with your opinion. Post your comment by *(insert deadline)*.

---

2   Once everyone has posted their comment, assign each student a number which will decide the order of posting. Then post Task 2 and set a deadline for posting all arguments.

▶ Task 2: Interaction

Here is that statement again:

Movie or music piracy online, if done by individuals, is not a serious crime.

1   Student 1 posts and should play devil's advocate to the statement. Write why you think online piracy is a serious crime, even if it's just individuals doing it.
2   Student 2 should play devil's advocate to the first person's post, and argue why online piracy is not a serious crime.
3   Continue this way until everyone has posted.

Here are some useful phrases for starting your post.

What (Student 1) said above may be true up to a point, but ...

That is a good point, however ...

On the other hand …

What (Student 2) said above is not really true. In fact …

But the truth of the matter is …

Post your arguments by *(insert deadline)*.

3 Allow everyone to post their 'devil's advocate'. At the end, wrap up the discussion by asking if there are really two sides to this story, or if students agree more with one or the other.

5.8 The lions' dilemma

Outline	Students are divided into two groups of lions and need to make choices on what action they will do without knowing what the other group decides. This activity works best in a synchronous environment.
Level	Upper intermediate and above (B2–C1)
Learning focus	Making suggestions
Time	30–45 minutes
Preparation	No advance preparation required.

Procedure

1 This stage can be done face-to-face or online. Set up a chat room and a time for this activity. Once students have arrived and you have greeted them, post Task 1.

🖑 Task 1: Stimulus

I'm going to divide you into two groups and send you to breakout rooms (a separate private chat room away from the others). I want you to imagine that you are each a group of lions in the savannah. The objective is to gain points.

You can gain points by choosing to rest or to hunt. For example, if Group A hunts and Group B rests then Group A gains 5 points and Group B loses 5 points. I will explain more in the breakout rooms.

---

2 Divide the group into two groups and send them to breakout rooms. Then visit each breakout room and post Task 2.

🖑 Task 2: Interaction

You are a group of lions on the savannah. You know there is another group of lions out there too.
The game is divided into turns. Each turn you must decide as a group what you will do: hunt or rest. If you hunt, you gain points in the form of food. If you sleep, you gain points in the form of rest.

However, there are limited resources on the savannah. Your choices will affect the other group. Here is how it works.

CHOICE		RESULT	
Lion Group A	Lion Group B	Lion Group A	Lion Group B
Rest	Rest	+3	+3
Rest	Hunt	−5	+5
Hunt	Rest	+5	−5
Hunt	Hunt	−3	−3

So, imagine you choose to hunt this turn. If the other group also chooses to hunt, you both lose 3 points (in this case you would have −3 points). But if the other group rests, then you gain 5 points and the other group loses 5 points!

If you both rest this turn, you both gain 3 points.

Now, you have five minutes to discuss among yourselves the best strategy. Then tell me if your group chooses to hunt or rest this turn.

The activity will last for seven turns and at the end we will count up the points. If you have negative points, your group of lions does not survive!

3 At the end of the five minutes, ask each group to report to you their choice. Then bring everyone back to the chat room and share the choices. Give the groups some time to discuss as a whole group (and maybe negotiate). Keep a record of the points, then send the groups back to the breakout rooms and repeat Task 2.

4 At the end of the activity, count up the points. Did both groups of lions survive or not? What did they learn about themselves during the activity?

Variation
After rounds 3 and 6, allow each group to send a 'negotiator' to meet in a third breakout room. They can communicate to each other and then report back to their group. If you do this, then do not allow the groups to communicate with each other in stage 4. The negotiators become the only mode of communication between the groups.

5.9 The latest greatest thing

Outline	Students argue for and against the use of a new technology among young people and then decide if it should get funding.
Level	Intermediate and above (B1–C1)
Learning focus	Giving opinions, discussing pros and cons of a new technology
Time	20–30 minutes per task over a week
Preparation	Think of a new technology that is somewhat controversial (e.g. a new form of communication, a new medical discovery, a new use for robots). The example below is for a new kind of messaging app. Prepare a similar description of your technology.

Procedure

1   Set up a forum and give it a title (e.g. *The latest greatest thing*). Post Task 1. If you are discussing a different kind of technology (see *Preparation* above), you will need to adjust this so that it reflects your choice. Set a deadline for posting answers.

▶ Task 1: Stimulus

Imagine the following situation.

A company has developed a new text messaging system called 'Hyde'. With Hyde, people can send anonymous text messages to anyone. This means that the person who receives the text message will not know who it comes from. Hyde also lets you set up private anonymous groups, and comes with an online public bulletin board which allows users to post anonymous messages. Hyde takes privacy very seriously and believes its anonymous messaging system to be the most secure.

The company is doing some market research. Here are their questions:

Would you be interested in using an app like this? Why / Why not?

What would you use it for?

How much would you pay for an app like this?

Would you use this app instead of other similar apps?

Post your answers to these questions by *(insert deadline)*.

---

2   Read the responses and make a note of any arguments against technology like this (e.g. it could be used for bullying). Then divide your students into three groups:
   - Group A are those in favour of the technology
   - Group B are those against it
   - Group C is made up of judges, who play the board of directors.

You can do this based on their original posts, or randomly. Students should ideally be in Group A or B depending how they answered the questions in Task 1. But if groups are very uneven in size then you may wish to balance them out. Then post Task 2. Again, you can adjust this to match points that came up relating to your choice of technology and student responses. Set a deadline for posting replies.

▶ Task 2: Interaction

Here is a message from the company that is creating Hyde, in response to your posts:

Thank you for your input into the Hyde message app! We see that some of you have concerns, mainly that (insert concerns or arguments that students had). We take these things very seriously at Hyde, and here's what we can do:

- *We can make it possible to block offending messages or a messenger.*
- *We will put a warning on the app that says you must not use it for bullying.*
- *We can let users report any problems or abuse to Hyde Headquarters.*
- *We can make the app free if we include advertisements.*

If we include these features, would you still be interested? Why / Why not?

You are going to work in three groups.

Group A: (*insert names of students*). You now think that Hyde is an interesting app.

Group B: (*insert names of students*). You still have doubts about the technology.

Group C: (*insert names of students*). Read the replies from Groups A and B.

Groups A and B, please post your replies to the company in the forum. You can all comment on what other people say here as well. Post your replies by (*insert deadline*).

3   Allow students to post reactions to the app and their arguments for and against now that they have read Hyde's proposed changes. After the deadline is up, post Task 3 for the judges in Group C and give them a deadline for posting their decision.

▶ Task 3: Decision

Thank you for your responses. The company is now going to ask for investment approval for their app. They need a YES or NO from the board of directors.

Group C, you are the board of directors. You need to decide if you are going to invest in the Hyde app. Read the arguments for and against from the users. Then post a short summary of these and your final decision. If you vote YES, then the app is approved. If you vote NO, the app will not get the money it needs and will not exist.

Post your decision by (*insert deadline*).

4   To wrap up the activity, thank everyone for their participation and congratulate them on finishing the tasks.

5.10 Debating a motion

Outline	Students work in groups and prepare a debate. They then take turns debating the motion in the forum.
Level	Upper intermediate and above (B2–C1)
Learning focus	Constructing an argument, agreeing and disagreeing (*I think that …, In my opinion …, Do you think …, What about …,* etc.)
Time	Two weeks
Preparation	Choose a motion for your students to debate. The example below is based on the motion 'Schools should ban homework.' You can find a list of motions online using the search term 'sample debate motions'.

Procedure

1   Divide your class into two groups, Group A and Group B. This activity works best in classes of six (two groups of three). If you have a large class, subdivide the class into two debates in different forums. If the number of students in your class will not divide by six, assign more than one student to each number in the two groups. Give the students in each group a number: A1, A2, A3 and B1, B2, B3.

2   Set up a forum and give it a title (e.g. *Debating a motion*). Post Task 1 to all students. Tell the students to research and prepare arguments in favour of their position. Set a deadline for preparing arguments.

Task 1: Stimulus

You are going to debate the following statement:

Schools should ban homework.

Group A: you are in favour of the motion.

Group B: you are against the motion.

You have until *(insert deadline)* to prepare your arguments. Then the debate will begin in this forum.

---

3   When the deadline is reached, post Task 2 and set deadlines for posting arguments, cross-examining and summarizing. Make sure each student knows their role. The first student in each group is responsible for posting the initial arguments, the second is responsible for cross-examining the other group, and the third is responsible for summarizing. Then run the debate.

Task 2: Interaction

You are now going to debate the motion. Here is how it works:
Student A1: you begin. Introduce the motion, and post your arguments in favour of it.
Student B1: post against the motion. Include your arguments against it.
Your arguments must be posted by *(insert deadline)*.

Student B2: you now cross-examine Student A1. Ask questions about their argument and try to find problems with it!
Student A2: you now cross-examine Student B1. Ask questions about their argument and try to find problems with it!

Your questions and answers must be finished by *(insert deadline)*.

Student A3: summarize the points made by your group and restate your position. Include criticism of the points made by the other group.
Student B3: summarize the points made by your group and restate your position. Include criticism of the points made by the other group.

Your summary must be finished by *(insert deadline)*.

---

4   At the end, ask students informally which arguments they thought were most compelling. If you had an odd number of students, you could assign one or two students as the judges. They have to decide which argument won and say why at the very end.

5.11 Create a constitution

Outline	Students suggest laws for an imaginary country, then read, comment on and vote on each other's laws.
Level	Intermediate and above (B1–C1)
Learning focus	Modals for permission and prohibition (*can, can't, must, mustn't, should, shouldn't*), other expressions for permission and prohibition (*be allowed to, be forbidden to, be illegal to*)
Time	15–30 minutes per task over a minimum of four days
Preparation	No advance preparation required.

Procedure

1 This stage can be done face-to-face or online. Have an introductory discussion with students on what is and is not allowed in different countries (e.g. driving at over 100 kph, voting at age 18).

If your students are from different countries you can ask a number of questions, e.g.:
At what age can you drive in your country?
At what age can you vote?
At what age can you get married?
When can you vote?

If they are from the same country make the questions into a quiz, e.g. *At what age can you drive in Chile?*

Tell students that they are going to invent laws for an imaginary country. Ask for suggestions for a name for the imaginary country.

2 Set up a forum and give it a title (e.g. *Create a constitution*). Post Task 1 and set a deadline for posting three laws.

Task 1: Stimulus

This week you will need to check in to this forum regularly. Begin by posting a rule or law for (*insert name of imaginary country*), e.g.:

It is illegal to keep dogs.

Post three laws by (*insert deadline*).

---

3 When the deadline is up, post Task 2 and ask students to vote on each other's laws. If your forum has a 'like' feature, they can vote by clicking on the 'like' button. Alternatively, you could set up a poll using a polling website (search online using the search term 'make your own poll') and use that. Set a deadline for posting comments and voting.

Task 2: Interaction

Read each other's laws and vote for any that you like. If a law gets three votes it is passed and becomes part of your country's constitution. You can:
- discuss the laws
- try to get votes
- pass other laws that undo previous laws.

You have until *(insert deadline)* to post laws, comment, discuss and vote.

4 Then go through the posts, collecting all the 'laws' with more than three votes. Copy and paste them into a document containing all the laws and post it with the title *Your constitution*.

5.12 Complete the sentence

Outline	Every 24 hours the teacher posts a sentence stem on a topic which the students must complete according to their own ideas and opinions.
Level	Intermediate and above (B1–C1)
Learning focus	*should, ought to*
Time	10–15 minutes per task over a week
Preparation	Choose an accessible topic that students are likely to have many views on (e.g. childhood, bringing up children, health, friendship, immigration, marriage). Prepare a series of sentence stems about the topic that could elicit different opinions and responses. See *Possible topics* with example sentence stems below.

Procedure

1 Set up a forum and give it a title (e.g. *Complete the sentence*). Post Task 1 and set a deadline 24 hours ahead. Allow a day for students to complete the sentence in their own way. They should enter the whole sentence. The example below uses a sentence about childhood.

Task 1: Stimulus

This week you will need to check in to this forum regularly. I will be posting the beginning of a sentence. Your job is to copy that beginning and complete it with your own idea. Write no more than the sentence in your post.

Every 24 hours I will post a new sentence stem, which you must complete. Your first sentence stem is:

It is important for children to …

Complete this sentence by *(insert deadline)*, e.g.:

It is important for children to know that their parents love them.

---

2 After the first 24 hours are up, post another sentence stem. Students repeat the process.

3 Continue in this way for four days or as many days as you have sentence stems.

4 Then post Task 2 and set a deadline for posting comments.

Task 2: Interaction

Choose one sentence stem that you find interesting. Look through your classmates' posts to see how they have completed the sentence. Write a summary and say what you think, e.g.:
Most of my classmates think that the secret of a happy childhood is love. One person thinks that money is also important. I agree that love is most important. Having a lot of money is not important, but having enough money to live is very important. If you have not got enough money to feed your children, then they will not have a happy childhood.

Post your comments by *(insert deadline)*.

---

5 To wrap up the activity, thank everyone for their participation and congratulate them on finishing the tasks.

Possible topics
Childhood
It is important for children to …
Parents should …
Schools and teachers ought to …
The secret of a happy childhood is …

Health
It is important to …
People should …
To stay healthy, older people ought to …
Governments should …
One of the greatest challenges to health in this country is …

5.13 Cause and consequence

Outline	Students work in pairs to brainstorm the causes and consequences of a statement about the future. They then discuss this and other statements in a forum.
Level	Intermediate and above (B1–C1)
Learning focus	Cause and result clauses (*as a result of, because, because of, in consequence, one reason for this is …, so, therefore*), agreeing and disagreeing (*I think that …, in my opinion …, do you think …, what about …,* etc.)
Time	30 minutes per task over a week
Preparation	No advance preparation required.

Procedure

1 Set up a forum and give it a title (e.g. *Cause and consequence*). Divide your class into pairs. Post Task 1 to all students and set a deadline.

Task 1: Stimulus

Imagine you live in 2050.
In this discussion you will be working in pairs. Your teacher will send each pair a statement about life in 2050. Email or set up a chat with your partner and make a list of:
- all the causes that led to this event/fact
- all the consequences of this event/fact.

Please post your causes and consequences in this forum by *(insert deadline)*.
Here is an example:

Fact: People live longer.
Causes:
This is because of improvements in health care.
One reason for this is better hygiene.
This is because of a rise in living standards.
This is as a result of improved safety standards in workplaces.

Consequences:
As a result, pension costs have increased.
So there is more competition for jobs.
This may mean that people have to work longer.
Healthcare costs have increased.

---

2 Send each pair one of the statements by private message. Set a deadline for posting causes and consequences.

Statements about life in 2050
The Sahara Desert has doubled in size.
There are no more private cars.
People are afraid to use social media.
More people live in gated communities.
People live longer.
There is a much greater difference in income between rich and poor people.
People are having fewer children.
The average temperature is 2 degrees hotter.

3   After the deadline is up, assign each pair another pair to work with (e.g. Students A and B work
    with Students C and D). Then post Task 2 and set a deadline for posting questions and answers.
    Each pair should go through the other pair's causes and consequences and find one or two which
    they query or challenge. They post their query as a reply to the original post.

    The authors of the original post should respond to the query or challenge either by defending their
    original viewpoint or conceding the point.

Task 2: Interaction

Your teacher will send you another group's post to look at in the forum. You can agree with, disagree with
or ask questions about this post. You must post at least one or two comments about it, e.g.:

*I agree that people will live longer because health care will improve but I don't think pension costs will
necessarily rise: people could work longer. Who do you think will pay for the pensions?*

Answer the questions the other students have asked you. Post your questions and answers by
(insert deadline).

---

4   At the end, read all the discussions. Which situations seem the most likely for 2050?

Variation
This forum format can be adapted to many different topics, e.g.:

Education
There will be more online teaching.
The price of tertiary education means that students are reluctant to start degrees.
Businesses may have a larger say in what students study.

Technology
Technology is evolving at a pace that has never been seen before.
There are great advances in artificial intelligence.
People are spending large amounts of time watching videos and interacting in virtual worlds.
Many members of the public are not well-informed about privacy issues.
Robots can make decisions, but it is difficult to create robots that make ethical decisions.

5.14 Yes, but …

Outline	Students research the advantages and disadvantages of various ideas around a given topic and argue about the merits of each.
Level	Upper intermediate and above (B2–C1)
Learning focus	Language of hypothesis and recommendation (*should, would*)
Time	Minimum three days (one to read, one to collaborate on arguments and one to argue)
Preparation	Find some background reading on ideas around your chosen topic and its advantages and disadvantages. Make a reading list for students. This activity template is adaptable to any topic with advantages and disadvantages (see *Variation*). The example topic here is climate change. For some of the other topics you may need to change the wording in the task boxes, e.g. *You are going to discuss the advantages and disadvantages of convenience foods.*

Procedure

1   This stage can be done face-to-face or online. Set up a forum and give it a title (e.g. *Yes, but …*). Set up two separate groups (private message groups, closed groups or chat rooms) within the forum and give them the titles *Advantages* and *Disadvantages*. Post a reading list of links to sources with Task 1. Ask each group to do some reading from the list you have posted and make arguments in favour of the advantages and disadvantages of each idea.

Task 1: Stimulus

You are going to discuss the advantages and disadvantages of various solutions to the issue of climate change.

First, read some material from the reading list and, working individually, make a list of solutions to the problem of climate change.

Advantages group: list all the advantages for each solution.

Disadvantages group: list all the disadvantages for each solution.

Make your lists of advantages and disadvantages by *(insert deadline)*. You will refer to these in Task 2.

---

2   When they have finished their reading and note-taking, post Task 2. Set a deadline for them to finish this preparatory discussion.

Task 2: Interaction

In your groups, share some of the arguments you have read that support your position.

Finish your discussion by *(insert deadline)*.

---

3   When the time limit has been reached, regroup the students in pairs so that each pair has one Advantage note-taker and one Disadvantage note-taker. Post Task 3 and set a deadline for finishing the discussion:
   • The Advantages should begin with a statement of their first proposed solution.
   • The Disadvantages should reply, beginning *Yes, but …* and stating a counter-argument.

- The Advantages should reply *Yes, but* ... with a further argument in favour of their solution.
- The Disadvantages can then voice further objections / raise further problems on the same topic. Each exchange after the initial recommendation should begin with *Yes, but* ...

Task 3: Interaction

Work in pairs: Advantages and Disadvantages.

The Advantages begin. Post a recommendation for a solution (one sentence), e.g.:
People should ....
To halt climate change we should ....
Climate change would be slowed down if ...

The Disadvantages reply, beginning *Yes, but* ... and stating a disadvantage, e.g.:
Yes, but if we did that, we would ...
Yes, but people wouldn't ...
Yes, but it would be difficult to ...

The Advantages reply *Yes, but* ... with another argument in favour of the solution.

The person who can continue with the *Yes, buts* for longest is the winner!

Finish your discussion by *(insert deadline)*.

---

4   When all the pairs have finished their discussions, bring everyone together in the main forum and find out which pair had the greatest number of exchanges. Congratulate them and ask them to publish their discussion in the main forum. Then invite any of the others to contribute to try and make it even longer!

Variation
This activity template can be adapted to many topics, e.g.:
- package holidays as opposed to do-it-yourself holidays
- convenience foods
- space exploration
- the Olympic Games being held in your country
- increased leisure time because of automation
- living in an apartment vs a house
- living in a city vs living in the country.

5.15 **Netiquette**

Outline	Students read a guide to etiquette and social behaviour written approximately 100 years ago and discuss which of the rules can be applied to online behaviour. They then collaborate to write a similar guide to 'netiquette'.
Level	Intermediate and above (B1–C1)
Learning focus	Imperatives, modals of obligation
Time	30–45 minutes over three days
Preparation	No advance preparation required.

Procedure

1   This stage can be done face-to-face or online. Ask students what they think of how people behave online. Are they generally well behaved or badly behaved? Can they think of examples when they have felt annoyed by people's online behaviour? When they have discussed this, tell them that in the following activity, they are going to think about and discuss 'netiquette' or appropriate behaviour online.

2   Set up a forum and give it a title (e.g. *Netiquette*). Then post Task 1 and set a deadline for posting comments.

▶ Task 1: Stimulus

In the early 20th century it was popular to talk about how to behave in public. This was called 'etiquette'. Here are some examples of rules for good etiquette.

Don't argue in public.
Don't be rude.
Don't make fun of other people's weaknesses or ignorance.
Don't talk about private family issues in public.
Don't say bad things about friends in public.
Don't get angry or lose your temper in public.
Don't make private letters public.
Nobody likes it when someone shows off.

Today, people talk about rules on how to behave online. This is called 'netiquette'. Look at the rules above. What advice would stay the same? Would you modify or change anything? Is anything not relevant any more?

Post your comments by *(insert deadline)*.

---

3   When they have posted comments and replies, post Task 2 and set a deadline for posting comments.

⬏ Task 2: Interaction 1

1 Look at your comments about what is still relevant today. How would you rewrite these points to make them apply to netiquette? For example, if you think, 'Don't get angry or lose your temper in public' is still relevant to online behaviour, how would you rewrite this so that it specifically applies to behaviour in emails and social media? One rewrite could be 'Don't flame people online' ('flaming' is posting insulting or offensive comments to someone online).

2 Discuss what extra rules you would add for a guide to 'netiquette'.

Post your comments by *(insert deadline)*.

4 Now ask students to look through the ideas posted in Task 2 and to select their top five rules. You can ask them to make a poster and post using an online curation tool.

⬏ Task 3: Interaction 2

Look through the discussion in Task 2. What are the top five rules for netiquette that you would choose? Choose five rules and make a poster.

Put up your poster by *(insert deadline)*.

6 Fanciful interaction

6.1 Almost superpower

Outline	Students take turns posting a superpower they have, and adding conditions to each other's superpowers. With higher levels this could be done synchronously in a chat room.
Level	Elementary and above (A2–C1)
Learning focus	Linkers to show contrast, *can/can't, be able to*
Time	10–15 minutes per task over three days
Preparation	No advance preparation required.

Procedure

1 This stage can be done face-to-face or online. Brainstorm a list of famous superheroes, and the powers that they have (e.g. *Superman can fly.*).

2 Set up a forum and give it a name (e.g. *Almost superpower*). Post Task 1 and set a deadline for posting superpowers and conditions.

Task 1: Stimulus

In this activity one person posts a superpower they would like to have, e.g.:

I can fly.

The next person has to add a condition to the superpower. You need to make it less powerful! Begin with the words *But you ...*, e.g.:

But you can only fly 1 metre off the ground.

Then add your own superpower in the same post. Then another person does the same. Continue until everyone has posted at least one superpower.

I'll begin:

I can fly!

Post your superpowers and conditions by *(insert deadline)*.

---

3 Let students post their superpowers and the stipulations to each other's superpowers. It is best to let this develop naturally, but if people are not posting then set up an order of names and prompt them.

4 At the end, create a summary of all the superpowers and their conditions. Ask students to vote on the best, funniest, most interesting one.

Variation

If students liked this 'blocking' game, you could repeat it but instead of superpowers, have them begin with the phrase *I have a lifetime supply of ...*, e.g.:

I have a lifetime supply of chocolate.

But you are allergic to chocolate. I have a lifetime supply of sunlight.

But you live underground ...

6.2 Alphabet expedition

Outline	Students take turns to post short descriptions of each of the 26 members on an expedition in the jungle to a lost temple, beginning each description with consecutive letters of the alphabet.
Level	Beginner and above (A1–C1)
Learning focus	Vocabulary of countries, likes and dislikes, hobbies and interests
Time	30 minutes per task over a week
Preparation	Find a picture of a temple in the jungle to put into the first post.

Procedure

1   Set up a forum for this task and give it a name (e.g. *Alphabet expedition*). Assign a student the letter A. Post the picture and Task 1. Set a deadline for posting each description.

▶ **Task 1: Stimulus and Interaction**

You are all adventurers on an expedition to discover a lost temple in the jungle. The expedition needs 26 people. You are going to decide who those people are. Read the instructions below.

The first person has the letter A. Please create a text like this, filling in each gap. All the gaps have to begin with the letter A.

His/Her name is A.................... and he/she is from A.................... . He/She likes a.................... but doesn't like a.................... . He/She eats a lot of a.................... .

When you finish, nominate another student to continue with the letter B.

You each have 24 hours to post your description, but try to do it more quickly! All descriptions should be posted by *(insert deadline)*.

---

2   Make sure that each student nominates a different student at the end of their post. If you have fewer than 26 students, some people can post twice or more.

3   If you see an erroneous suggestion, post a clarification but allow the activity to continue.

4   Every five or six letters, post a summary of the expedition so far by copying all the sentences and posting them in a single post. This will also help nudge the next person to post if they haven't already!

5   At the end, post the picture of the temple again and list the crew that the students have written. Thank the students for participating in the activity.

Variation

You could leave out the letters X and Q if you like from this activity and make the expedition 24 people instead. Another possibility for smaller groups is to give each student two or more letters.

A more advanced gap-fill text for higher levels could include gaps for character adjectives and emotions and action verbs, e.g.:

▶ The first person has the letter A. Please create a text like this. All the gaps have to begin with the letter A.

His/her name is A.................... and he/she is from A.................... . He/She likes a....................
but doesn't like a.................... . He/she eats a lot of a.................... . He/She is very
a.................... but not at all a.................... . He/She a....................s a lot and is often
a.................... .

When you finish, nominate another student to continue with the letter B.

6.3 Build a bio

Outline	Students look at a picture of a historical person and collaborate to write a fictitious biography. They then collaborate to find the real facts.
Level	Intermediate and above (B1–C1)
Learning focus	Past tenses, time expressions
Time	10 minutes for Task 1 and 20 minutes for Task 2 over a week
Preparation	Find a picture of a statue of a real historical person that students are unlikely to know. This could be a head of state of a different country, a sports person who was famous 100 years ago, someone famous in the arts, a lesser-known Roman emperor, etc.

Procedure

1   Set up a forum and give it a title (e.g. *Build a bio*). Post the picture and Task 1 to all students. Set a deadline for posting biographies.

Task 1: Stimulus

Look at the picture. You're going to create your own biography of this person. One person begins with a sentence like this:

(insert name) was a famous *(insert job, or reason they were famous)*.

The next person should copy and paste the first sentence and then continue with another sentence, e.g.:

He/She was born in *(insert year)*.

Continue like this, adding more and more to the biography until everyone has posted something about the person.

Your posts should be completed by *(insert deadline)*.

---

2   After the deadline is up, post Task 2 with a corrected version of the biography and the real name of the person. Copy the last person's post (which should have everyone's sentences), make any necessary corrections to the language that you see, and insert it into the Task 2 post. Set a deadline for posting responses.

Task 2: Interaction

Here is your completed biography, with some minor corrections I have made. Well done!

(insert complete biography here)

Now, this is the name of the real person: *(insert name here)*. How much information can you find out about him/her? Were any of the facts you wrote similar to the real story? Post a response here by *(insert deadline)*.

---

3   To wrap up the activity, thank everyone for their participation and congratulate them on finishing the tasks.

6.4 Fairy tale rewrite

Outline	The teacher posts a fairy tale, then changes one detail to make it more modern. Students follow suit, changing one detail at a time to modernize the fairy tale.
Level	Intermediate and above (B1–C1)
Learning focus	Narrative tenses
Time	2–3 days
Preparation	Find a modernized fairy tale that students are likely to know (optional). You could find these by doing an online search using the search term 'modernized fairy tale'.

Procedure

1   This stage can be done face-to-face or online. You could prepare for this by reading a modernized fairy tale with students.

2   Set up a forum with the title *Fairy tale rewrite*. Post Task 1 with a traditional fairy tale to the group. The example here is Cinderella. You can find the story on page 168.

▶ Task 1: Stimulus

Together we are going to take a traditional fairy tale and modernize it. First, read the traditional fairy tale.

(insert fairy tale)

---

3   Then post Task 2 and set a deadline for posting the complete story. Assign students an order for posting to ensure everyone gets a turn and the complete story is rewritten.

▶ Task 2: Interaction 1

Now take turns to change one detail at a time. Do this by copying the whole story and pasting it on this page. Then change the detail. Always copy the latest version of the story. Post by *(insert deadline)*.

Here is an example with the changed detail in **bold**. The next person to change a detail, copy this version and change another detail. Make your change in **bold**.

Not very long ago there was a girl called Cinderella, who lived with her stepmother and two stepsisters. The sisters were very ugly and the stepmother was very unkind. She made Cinderella do all the work in the house: the cooking and the cleaning and the washing. Cinderella was very unhappy with her life.

---

4   When everyone has posted and the story is transformed, you can continue the activity if you and the students wish, by asking them to find their own fairy tale, modernize it and post the story in the group. Begin by listing the new details that the students added to the story (e.g. vacuuming instead of cleaning the floors, a stretch limo instead of a coach and horses) and asking them to brainstorm other modern details that could change fairy tales (e.g. online shopping, social media). Post Task 3 and set a deadline for posting ideas.

▶ Task 3: Interaction 2

Here is a list of the modern details you put into Cinderella:

(insert list here)

What other modern inventions could you put into fairy stories to change them?

Post your ideas by *(insert deadline)*.

---

5   Then post Task 4, which asks students to choose a new story to modernize, and set deadlines for posting stories and comments.

▶ Task 4: Interaction 3

Find a different short fairy tale online.

Copy the story so that everyone can see the original. Then modernize some details and post the new story below the old one. Post your story by *(insert deadline)*.

Read other people's stories and comment on them.

What details have they changed?

Did the modern details make the characters' lives easier or more difficult?

Did they change the ending?

Post your comments by *(insert deadline)*.

---

6   You could print out the fairy tales and make a display or booklet for the students. Alternatively, you can put the stories on a wiki, ning or notice board using an online curation tool.

Variation

For higher-level students, you could give the students the main events instead of the full story. They then write the story collaboratively, adding in or changing details or actions. For example, Cinderella could be a student who has to work her way through college, she could meet the Prince at a speed-dating evening or he could search for her on social media.

▶ Cinderella story

Long long ago there was a girl called Cinderella, who lived with her stepmother and two stepsisters. The sisters were very ugly and the stepmother was very unkind. She made Cinderella do all the work in the house: the cooking and the cleaning and the washing. Cinderella was very unhappy with her life.

One day, a messenger came to the house with invitations to a party at the palace. The ugly sisters were delighted and started to plan what they would wear to the party, but the stepmother told Cinderella that she could not go because her clothes were too old and dirty and she had no shoes. On the evening of the party, the ugly sisters and the stepmother left in a coach in their beautiful party clothes. Cinderella sat alone in the kitchen, feeling very sad. Suddenly a woman appeared in the room. 'Who are you?' asked Cinderella, surprised. The woman replied, 'I am your fairy godmother. I have come to see why you are sad.' Cinderella said, 'I want to go to the party but my stepmother won't let me go.' The fairy godmother said, 'Don't cry! You shall go to the ball!' 'But look at my clothes!' said Cinderella. 'And I have no shoes!' The fairy godmother waved her wand and immediately Cinderella had a beautiful dress and glass slippers. Then she waved her wand again at a pumpkin that was on the kitchen table and at six mice near the cupboard. 'Come outside,' she said. They went out and there in the street was a golden carriage and four black horses, and two coachmen to drive the coach. Cinderella was so happy! She got into the coach and the fairy godmother said, 'But the magic will only last until midnight. You must leave the party before then.'

When Cinderella entered the palace, everybody thought how beautiful she was. Nobody, not even Cinderella's stepmother or stepsisters, recognized her because she looked so different. The handsome Prince Charming looked at her and fell in love with her straight away. He danced with her all night. At the last moment, Cinderella remembered her fairy godmother's words and ran out of the palace without a word to the prince. One of her glass slippers came off as she ran down the steps but Cinderella did not go back for it. She got home as the clock began to strike twelve. Her coach turned back into a pumpkin, the horses into mice and her beautiful dress into dirty rags.

Back at the palace everyone was talking about the beautiful girl who had left so suddenly. The prince wanted to find out who the beautiful girl was, and where she had gone, but he did not even know her name. On the palace steps he found the small glass slipper. The prince said, 'I will search for the girl whose foot fits this slipper and marry her!'

The next day, the prince and his servants took the glass slipper and started to visit every house in the country. But nobody's foot would fit in the slipper. Then they came to Cinderella's house. The ugly sisters tried on the little glass slipper but their feet were too big. Cinderella's stepmother refused to let her try on the slipper, but the prince said, 'Let her try on the slipper too!' Cinderella put the slipper on and everyone saw that it fitted her perfectly. So the prince married Cinderella and they lived together happily ever after.

6.5 Why?

Outline	The teacher posts a picture of a person or animal whose face or body language shows emotion, suggesting a reason why they feel that way. Students comment, suggesting alternative reasons. Then students find and post their own pictures and comment on each other's pictures in the same way.
Level	Lower intermediate and above (B1–C1)
Learning focus	Suggestions and giving reasons (*Maybe, Perhaps, I think, could, may, might*)
Time	10 minutes per task over 2–3 days
Preparation	Find a picture of a person or animal that appears to show emotion.

Procedure

1 This stage can be done face-to-face or online. Brainstorm with the students things or events that can cause people to be *happy, sad, angry* or *worried*. Set up a forum and give it a title (e.g. *Why?*). Post Task 1 along with your picture, suggesting a reason for the emotion. Ask students for alternative explanations. The example below is of a picture taken at Dublin Airport.

Task 1: Stimulus

These depressed people are at Dublin Airport. Suggest reasons why they might be feeing sad. Use language like *maybe … perhaps … could, may, might.*

I'll begin:

Maybe their plane is delayed.

Post your suggestion by *(insert deadline).*

---

2 When the deadline is up, post Task 2 and set a deadline for posting pictures and suggestions.

Task 2: Interaction

Now you! Find a picture of a person or animal looking sad, happy, worried, angry, fed up, etc. and post it. Suggest a reason why they might feel this way.

Then look at other people's pictures and suggest more reasons. Comment on at least three people's pictures.

Post your picture and suggestions by *(insert deadline)*.

3   To wrap up the activity, thank everyone for their participation and congratulate them on finishing the tasks.

6.6 Murder mystery

Outline	Students are given a scenario of a murder case. They are each given a clue about the night's events leading up to the time the murder was committed. They speculate about who could have committed the crime, then use the evidence to decide the murderer, the motive and how the crime was committed.
Level	Intermediate and above (B1–C1)
Learning focus	Speculation and deduction: *could have, might have, must have, may have, can't have* + past participle
Time	Minimum two days
Preparation	No advance preparation required.

Procedure

1 Private message each student one numbered clue. If you have fewer students than the number of clues, combine some clues so that the number of clues matches the number of students. Tell students they are going to work together to solve a murder mystery and they should not share these clues with each other at this stage.

▶ Private message clues

1 There were no fingerprints on the knife.

2 There were some drops of liquid on the floor.

3 The couple and guests had dinner together in the dining room. Dinner finished at 10 o'clock.

4 After dinner John, Tom and Marie went to the living room to watch the news.

5 At 10 o'clock, Marion cleared the table and went into the kitchen to wash up.

6 Paul did not join the others in the living room but went into the study, saying he had to answer a couple of emails. He took a cup of coffee with him.

7 Amy went with Marion into the kitchen at 10 o'clock to help with the washing up. Marion washed the dishes and she started drying them.

8 Paul's coffee cup was empty and lying on its side.

9 At 10:25, John called Amy into the living room to watch a news item. As she left the kitchen Marion's cellphone buzzed and she picked it up to read the message.

10 At 10:25, Marie went upstairs to get a book from her room. She passed Amy in the hall.

11 Just before 10:30, Tom said he was tired and was going to bed.

12 At 10:35, after the news item, Amy went back to the kitchen but found Marion had finished the washing-up and was pulling off her rubber gloves.

13 Marie came out of her room with a book in her hand at 10:30. She stopped to chat to Tom who was at the top of the stairs.

14 The liquid on the study floor was water.

15 Amy and Marion went to the living room to join John just after 10:35.

16 Marie Smith doesn't have a cellphone.

17 The message on Marion's cellphone said: 'Marie, I've decided to alter my will. I must see you tomorrow. Paul.'

18 Paul's lawyer is called Marie Smith.

---

2 Set up a forum and give it a title (e.g. *Murder mystery*). Post Task 1.

▶ Task 1: Stimulus

Here is the scenario. I will send you your instructions in a few minutes.

The murder happened in the house of Paul and Marion Brown. Paul was found dead in his study. He had been stabbed with a carving knife. He was found at 11 o'clock by his wife. The police put the time of the murder at 10:30 pm. That evening the Browns had four guests staying with them: their old friends Amy and John Jones, Marion's brother, Tom Crowe, and a school friend of Marion's, Marie Smith.

---

3 Shortly afterwards post Task 2 and set a deadline for posting solutions.

▶ Task 2: Interaction

Everyone has a numbered clue. You must post these in order. The student with Clue number 1 should begin.

Post your clue. Everyone should read the clue and post deductions and suggestions. As an example, here is a clue and deductions that are not connected with our story:

Clue X: *The window was open.*

Possible posts:

The murderer might have got in through the window.

Or he might have come in through the door but left through the window.

Or he could have come in through the window and left through the door.

But if he did that, he could have closed the window. So it is more likely that he left through the window.

When there has been some discussion of Clue 1, then the student with Clue 2 can post. Your own clue may help you work out what happened, but you may only discuss the clues that have been posted! It may help you to keep a chart of what happened and when:

10 pm	
10:25 pm	
10:30 pm	
10:35 pm	

Continue like this until the last clue has been posted. Then look back over all the clues and discuss them in order to fill in the following:

Murderer: ....

Motive: ....

How the murderer committed the crime: ....

Post your solution by *(insert deadline)*.

Monitor the postings to make sure the students are posting clues in the right order and that they are discussing each clue before going on to the next.

4   When they have come up with a solution, post Task 3 and set a deadline for posting.
    Invite comments.

⬉ Task 3: Solution

Read the solution below and comment: Is the solution the same as the one you came up with?

Murderer: The only person who could have committed the crime is Marion. The others all have alibis: Marie saw Amy crossing the hall and going into the living room at 10:25. John and Amy were together in the living room from 10:25 until 10:35. Tom and Marie saw each other upstairs at 10:30, the time of the murder.

Motive: Paul was contacting his lawyer Marie Smith, but mistakenly sent the message to Marion instead of Marie. Marion killed him to stop him changing the will.

How: After Amy left the kitchen, Marion read the message then took a knife from the washing-up, went to the study and stabbed her husband. The water on the floor was from the wet knife and there were no fingerprints because she kept her rubber gloves on. She returned to the kitchen, where Amy found her at 10:35.

Post your comments by *(insert deadline)*.

---

5   When everyone has commented, end the activity and thank students for their participation.

6.7 I wish I had a picture of …

Outline	Students post a sentence beginning *I wish I had a picture of …* and a reason. The first person to post a suitable picture continues the chain by posting a wish and a reason. This activity can be done in a synchronous or asynchronous environment.
Level	Intermediate and above (B1–C1)
Learning focus	Expressing wishes and giving reasons (*because, in order to, as, since*)
Time	30 minutes (synchronous), 10 minutes per task over 2–3 days (asynchronous)
Preparation	No advance preparation required.

Procedure

1 This stage can be done face-to-face or online. Discuss with students what kind of pictures they like in their home, in art galleries, in advertising and online. Set up a forum and give it a title (e.g. *I wish I had a picture of…*).

2 Post Task 1. If you are carrying out this activity asynchronously, set a deadline for posting pictures and requests. Then post your own wish, e.g. *I wish I had a picture of a Siamese cat. This is because I had a Siamese cat when I was a child and I miss her!*

Task 1: Stimulus

I'm going to post a request for a picture. Post a picture in reply.

The first person to post that picture must then post another request and the reason you want that picture. Write a sentence like this:

I wish I had a picture of ………………………… because / so that / in order to / since / as ………………………… .

For example:

I wish I had a picture of a strawberry cake as I am feeling hungry!

I wish I had a picture of flowers because it is winter and there are none in my garden!

My request:

I wish I had a picture of a Siamese cat. This is because I had a Siamese cat when I was a child and I miss her!

---

3 Now post Task 2 and set deadlines for replying and posting comments.

Task 2: Interaction

Now respond to the people who posted pictures for you, e.g.:

Student A: *I wish I had a picture of a strawberry cake as I am feeling hungry!*

Student B: *Here's a strawberry cake!*

Student A: *Thank you – that cake looks delicious!*

Student B: *You're welcome. I wish I had a picture of flowers because it is winter and there are none in my garden!*

Student C: *Here are some flowers!*

Student D: *Thanks for the flowers – they cheered me up and reminded me of summer!*
        And so on.

Post your replies by *(insert deadline)*.

Then look through all the pictures. Comment on any you like particularly, e.g.:

What a beautiful sunset!

That cat reminds me of my cat!

Post your comments by *(insert deadline)*.

If more than one person gave you a picture, make sure you respond to everyone.

---

4   To wrap up the activity, thank everyone for their participation and congratulate them on finishing the tasks. Collect and correct any useful errors or good examples of language that came up in the activity.

6.8 Magic market

Outline	Students take the role of various fairy tale characters with problems. They each have a charm or spell which will help with a particular problem – but not their own! They have to bargain and trade spells to obtain a spell which will help them. This activity can be done in a synchronous or asynchronous environment.
Level	Intermediate and above (B1–C1)
Learning focus	First conditional, suggestions (*How about …*)
Time	30 minutes (synchronous), 1–2 days (asynchronous)
Preparation	Familiarize yourself with the fairy tales Rapunzel, Cinderella, Jack and the Beanstalk, Hansel and Gretel, Sleeping Beauty and Snow White. You can find them online using the search term 'fairy tales'.

Procedure

1 This stage can be done face-to-face or online. Familiarize students with the fairy tales. Many of these have been made into films which the students may have seen in childhood even if the stories are not part of their culture. You could show them the trailers. The activity will work even if you do not have time for this stage and the students do not know the fairy tales, as background information is given in the role cards.

2 You can play this game in groups of four (with either the first four role cards or the last four role cards) or eight (with all cards). Groups of four will find a solution more quickly than a group of eight. Do not form groups with fewer than four. If there are fewer than eight students in a group, reassign the 'charms' so that there is one for everyone in the group (see *Solution* for the correct charms for each character). Structure the activity so that all problem posts take place in the main forum, and all offers of charms and exchanges take place by private message.

3 Set up a forum and give it a title (e.g. *Magic market*). When you have set up the groups, post Task 1 with the rules and check that students understand what they have to do.

⬛ Task 1: Stimulus 1

You are a fairy tale character with a problem! For example, you are Rapunzel:

You are locked in a high tower and cannot get out.

You have a charm but it is useless for your problem.

However it will help someone else with their problem!

You must give away your charm and get the charm that you need.

Rules

1 You cannot just give your charm to someone. You have to exchange so that you receive one in return.

2 If their charm is useless to you, you can refuse to exchange and go on looking.

3 You can do 'intermediate deals', e.g.:

Rapunzel has the charm that Jack needs.

Jack has the charm that Snow White needs.

Snow White has the charm that Rapunzel needs.

Rapunzel will not exchange charms with Jack – she wants him to give her the charm that she needs. So Jack does an 'intermediate deal' with Snow White: he exchanges charms with her. Now Snow White is happy – she has the charm that she needs. And Jack is happy. He now has the charm Rapunzel needs so he can exchange charms with her. This makes Rapunzel happy too!

4   Private message each student with their role. You can find all the roles on page 179. Then post Task 2 and set a deadline for posting descriptions.

▶ Task 2: Stimulus 2

When you have got your role, you can begin the game.

Post in the main forum. Say who you are and describe your problem. Don't just copy and paste, and add some details to the problem, e.g.:

My stepmother hates me because I am prettier than she is.

Say how you feel, e.g.:

How can I find that girl? I don't even know her name. I feel desperate!

Don't say what charm you have! Just describe your situation.

Post your description by *(insert deadline)*.

---

5   When everyone has posted, post Task 3 asking them to begin to try and do exchange deals to get the charm they want. They should conduct these deals by private message. If you want to see what students are saying in their messages (e.g. for later error correction and feedback, or just to make sure the activity is working), add the instruction *Please include me in each message*. Set a deadline for posting results.

▶ Task 3: Interaction

When everyone has posted their problems, you can begin to offer to exchange charms. Do this by private message, not in the main forum, e.g.:

Student A: *Hey Snow White, I think I can help you! I have a charm to get rid of poison. How can you help me? Sleeping B.*

Student B: *Hi Beauty! I have a magic mirror. SW*

Student A: *That's no good to me! I need to get rid of this curse and wake up. If you can find a curse charm for me, then I can give you my charm.*

Who will be the first to get a useful charm?

When you get your charm, post in the main forum. Say what charm you got, how it has helped you, why you are happy and what you are doing now.

Post your results by *(insert deadline)*.

---

6   When all students have their charms and have posted to say how it has changed their lives, you can check that everyone got the right charm.

Solution

Rapunzel: magic ladder. This will help you escape from the tower.

Frog Prince: princess's kiss. This will turn you into a prince again.

Jack: goose that lays golden eggs. This will make you rich.

Gretel: finding the way spell. This will help you get out of the forest.

Hansel: slenderizing potion. This will make you thin so you can get out of the cage.

Sleeping Beauty: curse neutralizer. This will wake you up from your sleep.

Snow White: poison antidote. This means you will be alive again.

Prince Charming: magic GPS mirror. This will tell you where to find Cinderella.

Role cards for Magic market

 Rapunzel

You are a princess locked in a high tower. You want to escape and meet a prince who has asked you to marry him. You have a secret charm, but it is no use to you.

Your charm: a small box containing a princess's kiss. The kiss will change you into your former self.

 Frog Prince

You are a prince transformed into a frog by a wicked witch. You want to be a prince again and find a princess to marry you. You have a secret charm, but it is no use to you.

Your charm: you have a goose that lays golden eggs. It will make the owner rich for ever.

 Jack

You and your family are very poor. You have sold everything you own and have no money left. You have a secret charm, but it is no use to you.

Your charm: a spell that can help you find your way when you are lost.

 Gretel

You are a child who is lost in the forest. You want to find your way out. You have a secret charm, but it is no use to you.

Your charm: a magic ladder. It folds up into your pocket but you can make it as long as you like.

 Hansel

You are a child locked in a cage by a wicked witch. You want to escape but cannot squeeze through the bars. You have a secret charm, but it is no use to you.

Your charm: a curse neutralizer. If a fairy has put a curse on you, this charm will remove it.

 Sleeping Beauty

You are a princess. A fairy put a curse on you and now you are asleep for 100 years. You want to wake up. You have a secret charm, but it is no use to you.

Your charm: an antidote to poison.

 Snow White

Your wicked stepmother gave you a poisoned apple. You took a bite and fell into a deep sleep. If you swallow it, you will die. You don't want to die! You have a secret charm, but it is no use to you.

Your charm: a magic GPS mirror that can show past events, identify the people in them and tell you where to find them now.

 Prince Charming

You met a beautiful girl at a party. But she left before you could ask her to marry you. You want to find her – but you don't even know her name! You have a secret charm, but it is no use to you.

Your charm: a slenderizing potion that can make people thin.

6.9 My cupcake!

Outline	Students compete for a virtual cupcake by distracting each other. They get the cupcake if they are the first to distract the cupcake holder. Then other students try to distract them and get the cupcake in turn. With higher levels, this activity will work in a synchronous environment (chat room).
Level	Elementary and above (A2–C1)
Learning focus	Describing actions
Time	10–15 minutes per task over three days
Preparation	No advance preparation required.

Procedure

1   This stage can be done face-to-face or online. Ask students to list their favourite sweet foods or desserts and decide on one of these for the activity.

2   Create a forum and give it a name (e.g. *My cupcake!*). Post Task 1 along with a picture of the food you chose in the *Preparation* stage. The example uses a cupcake.

Task 1: Stimulus and Interaction

In this activity we are going to play a game. Here is a picture of a cupcake.

In the game you all want the cupcake. You must distract the person who has the cupcake and then say *My cupcake!*

Here are some example distractions to give you ideas:

I come up quietly behind you and take the cupcake. My cupcake!

I make a loud noise and you jump. I take the cupcake. My cupcake!

A beautiful bird flies past you and you look. I take the cupcake. My cupcake!

You cannot post two times in a row. Everyone has to try and take the cupcake at least two times! The activity will finish on *(insert deadline)*.

---

3   Let students post their distractions. It's best to let this develop naturally, but if people are not posting then set up an order of names and prompt them.

4   At the end, post a summary of all the distractions and make any language corrections you feel necessary. Congratulate the participants, and tell them they have ALL earned a cupcake.

6.10 Space tourists

Outline	Students act as either alien visitors or inhabitants of Earth. The aliens query various aspects of life on Earth that they do not understand and the inhabitants attempt to explain them.
Level	Elementary and above (A2–C1)
Learning focus	Asking for and giving explanations
Time:	Minimum two days (one to post and one to reply), preferably a week
Preparation	For higher-level students, find the poem *A Martian Writes A Postcard Home* by Craig Raine. For lower-level students, find some sci-fi pictures of cities on other planets.

Procedure

1 This stage can be done face-to-face or online.

For higher-levels students, introduce them to the poem *A Martian Writes A Postcard Home* by Craig Raine. Ask if they can identify the objects or phenomena that the Martian is puzzled about (books, mist, rain, car, watch or clock, telephone, bathroom, sleep and dreams).

For lower-level students, show them the pictures or post them online. Ask students: *What questions would you ask the inhabitants of these places?*

2 Set up a forum and give it a title (e.g. *Space tourists*). Tell students they are working on a fictitious website called EarthAnswers. This was set up to help space tourists from Mars and other planets who are confused and have some questions about life on Earth. They should try and explain the things they are puzzled about. Post Task 1 and set a deadline for posting explanations.

▶ Task 1: Stimulus

You are working on a website called EarthAnswers. This was set up to help space tourists from other planets who are confused and have some questions about life on Earth. You should try and explain the things they are puzzled about.

Here are your first questions:

Why do you keep people in prison in a box in your living room and why are they always fighting? Why do families sit and watch the people in the box while they fight? And why do they spend so many hours a day watching them?

Try to give a full explanation of all parts of the query.

Post your explanations by *(insert deadline)*.

---

3 When students have posted explanations, you have two options. With lower-level students, you could simply post more questions (Task 2a). Set a deadline for posting answers.

▶ Task 2a: Interaction

Here are some more questions from the space tourists:

Why are there so many rooms in your houses? Why do you need them?

Why do people travel everywhere in small metal boxes? Wouldn't it be better to have a big box for everyone? And why don't they fly?

Why do you keep animals to eat? Wouldn't it be better just to take pills?

I have seen water coming out of people's eyes. What is happening? Are they sick? Can you cure this or stop it happening?

Choose one or more questions to answer. Try to give a detailed explanation.

Post your answers by *(insert deadline)*.

Alternatively, with higher-level students, divide the students into two groups: Space tourists and EarthAnswers staff. Post each group a different role card. The space tourists should post questions similar to the example in Task 1, and the EarthAnswers team should try to explain. Set a deadline for posting and replying to questions.

▶ Task 2b: Interaction 1

Role card 1: Space tourists

You are visiting Earth from another planet. This is the first time you have been to Earth and you have a lot of questions about the things you have seen. Post your questions to EarthAnswers. Here are some of the things you might ask about:
- hospitals
- farming
- television
- anger
- war
- crying
- gambling
- cars.

Use your own ideas too!

Post your questions by *(insert deadline)*.

▶ Task 2b: Interaction 2

Role card 2: EarthAnswers team

Your job is to reply to puzzled space tourists explaining things they do not understand about life on Earth. Read their questions and choose some to answer.

Post your answers by *(insert deadline)*.

---

4   Thank everyone for their participation and congratulate them on finishing the tasks. Collect and correct any useful errors or good examples of language that came up in the activity.

6.11 Time travellers

Outline	Students imagine a time in the past they would like to travel back to. They post three facts about that time period. Others guess which period it is and then post questions for them to answer.
Level	Elementary and above (A2–C1)
Learning focus	Present simple, past simple
Time	2–3 days
Preparation	No advance preparation required.

Procedure

1 This stage can be done face-to-face or online. You could begin this activity with a clip from a film about time travel and ask students whether they would like to be able to travel in time.

2 Set up a forum and give it a title (e.g. *Time travellers*). Post Task 1 asking students to choose a period they would like to travel back to. They should post three facts about this period, without identifying the period. The others should try to guess which period it is (the example below is Ancient Egypt). Set a deadline for posting guesses.

Task 1: Stimulus

You have been given the power of time travel! Choose a period in history you would like to travel back to. Research three facts about this period and post them, e.g.:

In this period people worshipped cats.

People built huge buildings to bury their kings.

They invented a system of writing in pictures.

Then try to guess the historical period everyone else has chosen.

Post your guess by *(insert deadline)*. Answer people's guesses.

---

3 When everyone has guessed, post Task 2 and set a deadline for posting questions and answers.

Task 2: Interaction 1

Now imagine everyone has returned from their time travel experience. Choose one person and ask three questions. If someone has already asked questions, choose someone else.

1 Ask a factual question about life in that time period, e.g. *What did the Egyptians write on?*
2 Ask them to tell you about an incident (funny, embarrassing, frightening, etc.) that happened, e.g. *What happened when you first arrived – where were you and what did people say/do?*
3 Ask them about any problems time travel causes, e.g. *How does your family feel when you time travel?*

Use your imagination to answer the questions! Post questions and answers by *(insert deadline)*.

---

4   If you want to follow this activity up, you could ask students to use what they wrote in the online activity to write up their answers to a newspaper interview. Use this framework:

Task 3: Interaction 2

Last week our intrepid time traveller *(insert name)* travelled to *(insert time period)*. We interviewed him/her about their impressions.

(insert name), what are some of the things you found out about life in *(insert time period)*?

Tell us an anecdote about what happened there.

Time travel is fascinating, but does it cause any problems with life back in the 21st century?

---

5   You could collate answers and make a newspaper feature on time travel and post it online or make a poster for the classroom.

Variation

1   Ask students to choose a year (or assign one) in which a famous historical event occurred and post a message as if they were there. Other students guess where they are.

2   Instead of posting facts in Task 1, post the following:

Task 1: Stimulus

You have travelled backwards in time. Describe the place you're in and what you can see and hear.

Then try to guess the historical period everyone else has chosen.

Post your guess by *(insert deadline)*.

6.12 Rumour mill

Outline	Students each have a role card detailing some personal information about their character and the village where they live, together with a piece of gossip they have heard. They interact in pairs to pass on the gossip, but also to correct any rumours they hear which are incorrect. Finally they come together in a group forum to establish which rumours are false and find the one rumour that is true. This activity works better in a synchronous environment.
Level	Intermediate and above (B1–C1)
Learning focus	Past simple and continuous, present simple and continuous, reported speech
Time	20 minutes each for Tasks 1 and 2
Preparation	No advance preparation required.

Procedure

1   This stage can be done face-to-face or online. Set up a forum with a private message or chat facility, so that in Task 1 students can communicate privately without the whole group seeing what they write. Give the forum a title (e.g. *Rumour mill*). Prepare them for the task by asking about their experience of gossip: was the news they heard true or untrue?

You need a minimum of eight students for this game. For larger groups, up to 15, add the extra cards (see page 188). For groups over 16, play in two groups.

2   Private message each student a role card (see page 187).

3   Post Task 1 with a map of Little Whispers, showing where people live. Set a 20-minute deadline for posting gossip and reactions to other people's gossip. If you want to see what students are saying in their messages (e.g. for later error correction and feedback, or just to make sure the activity is working), add the instruction *Please include me in each message*.

▶ Task 1: Stimulus

This is a map of Little Whispers, a small village, showing where people in the village live.

In this role play you are all villagers living in Little Whispers. Your role card gives you some information about your character and also some gossip about another person in the village.

1   Private message one other person from the group. Start your message with your name from your role card, then tell them your gossip and listen/react to their gossip, e.g.:
    Student A: *I'm Hazel. I heard that Joanna was moving to London!*
    Student B: *I'm Matt. Oh no! I'll miss her. I heard that a hotel chain is going to build a big hotel here.*
    Student A: *That will really change the village.*

2   When you have finished, private message someone else. Tell them your gossip and someone else's gossip, e.g.:
    Student A: *I heard that Joanna was moving to London. And Matt told me some terrible news – a hotel chain is going to build a big hotel here!*
    Student C: *Well, there could be more jobs.*

If you hear some gossip about yourself which is not true, correct it! If it is true, keep quiet – maybe you don't want everyone to know!

You have 20 minutes to exchange all your gossip. The gossip above is just an example – your gossip is different!

4   When the time is up, post Task 2. Set a deadline of 20 minutes.

▶ Task 2: Interaction

Now post in the group forum.

Post any gossip you have heard, both if you think it is true and if you have heard that it isn't true, e.g.:

(Student A) and (Student B) told me that Joanna was moving to London, but Joanna says that's not true – she is just going to visit her sister for a month.

There is one piece of gossip that is true. Which is it?

5   When everyone has posted, make any necessary corrections to the language and check how many students identified the true piece of gossip (Alex is getting married).

Main role cards for Rumour mill

Joanna

You share a house with your friend Rose. You are close to your family, but recently you met a member of your family that you had never seen before: your uncle Jim, who lives in America. He came over to Britain and came to visit you. He took you for a meal in the village café.

Rumour: The village is lucky to have a small shop, but you have just heard that the shopkeeper, Peter, and his wife are leaving and the shop is closing down! This is bad news for the village!

Anna

You live with your husband Tom. You are very excited at the moment by the news that you are about to become an aunt. Your sister is having a baby. Yesterday you went to buy some baby clothes for a present for her.

Rumour: There is a young woman, Alice, opposite you in the village. A lot of different people seem to be going in and out of her house – you wonder what is happening!

Alex

You live on your own but two weeks ago you met a wonderful girl, Sue. Yesterday you asked her to marry you and she said yes!

Rumour: One thing disturbs you – the couple next door, Tony and Jane, are always shouting. You can hear their loud voices through the wall. You wonder what is happening.

Susie

You are a lodger with Mary, a nice older woman. You are a nurse and work nights at the moment, which means you get home about 5 am. You try to be as quiet as possible but you sometimes think you wake up the man in the house opposite.

Rumour: You saw Joanna who lives next to you in the café recently. She is single but she was with a man who was buying her a meal so you think she has a new boyfriend – he is much older than her. He sounded American.

Steve

You live with your wife, Amy. You don't have much money and your house needs repairing. But last week you won an expensive new car in a raffle. You don't really need such a flash car so you are planning to sell it to pay for the house repairs.

Rumour: The girl opposite, Susie, has a really wild social life. She must be partying every night! She goes out late and often wakes you up at 5 am when she comes home.

Jane

You live with your husband, Tony. You have both just joined a local dramatic society and are rehearsing for a play. You play a couple who are always shouting. You rehearse a lot at home.

Rumour: Yesterday you saw Alex, who lives next door to you, in a jeweller's shop in town. He was buying a ring. You think he must be getting married – but no one has ever seen his girlfriend!

Alice

You live on your own. You have a nice house, but you are a bit lonely in the village so you have decided to move into town where you have more friends. You are going to sell your house, so a lot of estate agents have been coming round to value the house.

Rumour: Exciting news! Yesterday in town you saw Anna, who lives opposite you. She was in a shop buying baby clothes. She must be pregnant!

Peter

You live with your wife, Sally. You own the village shop and have been the shopkeeper for many years. Recently you have decided to spend a couple of years travelling round the world. The shop isn't going to close though: your son is coming down to run it while you are away.

Rumour: Steve and his wife, Amy, live near you. They don't have much money. Their house really needs repairing. But yesterday you saw him in a flash new car! It must have been very expensive. You wonder where he got the money. Perhaps he stole it?

Extra role cards for Rumour mill

 Rose

You share a house with your friend Joanna. Just recently Joanna's Uncle Jim came to visit her and took her for a meal in the village café. It was a really special meeting because it was the first time she had ever met him, because he lives in America. Her family means a lot to her so she was very happy!

Rumour: The village is lucky to have a small shop, but you have just heard that the shopkeeper, Peter, and his wife are leaving and the shop is closing down! This is bad news for the village!

 Tom

You live with your wife, Anna. Anna is very excited at the moment by the news that she is about to become an aunt. Her sister is having a baby. Yesterday she went to buy some baby clothes for a present for her. And now she talks about babies all the time.

Rumour: There is a young woman, Alice, opposite you in the village. A lot of different people seem to be going in and out of her house – you wonder what is happening!

Mary

You have a lodger, Susie, a nice girl. She is a nurse and works nights at the moment, which means she gets home about 5 am. You are a bit deaf, so this doesn't bother you!

Rumour: You saw Joanna, who lives next to you, in the café recently. She is single but she was with a man who was buying her a meal so you think she has a new boyfriend – he is much older than her. He sounded American.

Amy

You live with your husband, Steve. You don't have much money and your house needs repairing. But last week Steve won an expensive new car in a raffle. You don't really need such a flash car so you are planning to sell it to pay for the house repairs.

Rumour: The girl opposite, Susie, has a really wild social life. She must be partying every night! She goes out late and often wakes you up at 5 am when she comes home.

Tony

You live with your wife, Jane. You have both just joined a local dramatic society and are rehearsing for a play. You play a couple who are always arguing. You rehearse a lot at home.

Rumour: Yesterday you saw Alex, who lives next door to you, in a jeweller's shop in town. He was buying a ring. You think he must be getting married – but no one has ever seen his girlfriend!

Freda

Your friend Alice lives in the village. She's a bit lonely – you always thought it was crazy to move there! Anyway, finally she has decided to move back into town to be near all her friends. She is going to sell her house, so a lot of estate agents have been coming round to value the house.

Rumour: Alice is very excited that her neighbour Anna is pregnant! Must be a boring village if that is exciting news!!

Sally

You live with your husband, Peter. You own the village shop and have been the shopkeepers for many years. Recently you have decided to spend a couple of years travelling round the world. The shop isn't going to close though – your son is coming down to run it while you are away.

Rumour: Steve and his wife, Amy, live near you. They don't have much money. Their house really needs repairing. But yesterday you saw him in a flash new car! It must have been very expensive. You wonder where he got the money. Perhaps he stole it?

From *Interaction Online* © Cambridge University Press 2017   PHOTOCOPIABLE

6.13 Disappearing act

Outline	Students have a diary showing what Harry was going to do yesterday, his birthday. They also each have role cards with descriptions of what actually happened on the birthday from people who know Harry. They must put these together to find what actually happened, and finally answer a quiz which will reveal Harry's whereabouts and who he was with.
Level	Intermediate and above (B1–C1)
Learning focus	Narrative tenses, *be going to*
Time	2–3 days
Preparation	No advance preparation required.

Procedure

1   This stage can be done face-to-face or online. Post Task 1. Tell students this was Harry's diary for yesterday, his birthday. You can discuss with them what would be their ideal birthday. What might Harry not like about his birthday?

> ▶ **Task 1: Stimulus**
>
> **Harry's diary**
>
> | | |
> |---|---|
> | 8 am | Breakfast meeting at work |
> | 10 am | Dentist's appointment |
> | 1 pm | Lunch with Will |
> | 4 pm | Tennis with Ian |
> | 6 pm | Drink with Mark |

---

2   Private message each student one numbered role card (see page 192). All the role cards should be used. If you have fewer than 16 students, message more than one role card to each student. If you have more than 16 students, play in two groups. Monitor to make sure they discuss what might have happened after each post. The first couple of times you may need to prompt a little, e.g. *So what do you think happened? Why do you think he wasn't there?*

3   Set up a forum and give it a name (e.g. *Disappearing act*). Post Task 2 to all students and set a deadline for posting ideas and completing the discussion.

> ▶ **Task 2: Interaction**
>
> You have Harry's diary for yesterday, his birthday. Your task is to find out what he actually did that day. You will all have a number and a role card. Read your role card and be prepared to expand the notes and post as if you are that person. For example, if your role card says:
>
> *Sam: Harry's friend. I knocked on his door at 9 am to give him a present. He wasn't there.*
>
> You could write: *I'm Sam, Harry's friend. I knocked on his door at 9 am because I had a present to give him …*
>
> You can add more details if you like, e.g.:
>
> *I'm Sam, Harry's friend from school. It was his birthday yesterday so I went round to see him at 9 am with a present for him …*

Student 1 posts first. Then everyone can discuss what might have happened, e.g.:

But Harry had a breakfast meeting at 8 am. That's why he wasn't at home.

He had a dentist's appointment at 10 am – perhaps he was on his way there.

When the discussion is finished, Student 2 can post.

Complete your discussion by *(insert deadline)*.

4   After the final post and discussion, post Task 3. See who can be the first to solve the puzzle. Set a deadline for posting the solution. After they have solved the puzzle, post the answers and get them to discuss the story of what happened that day.

▶ Task 3: Puzzle

Where did Harry go? Who did he meet?

Fill the blanks to find out. The first letter of each word will give you the answers.

Where:

1	What did Sam want to give Harry?	a _ _ _ _ _ _ _
2	What did he phone to cancel?	an _ _ _ _ _ _ _ _ _ _
3	Some friends wanted to pick Harry up at 12:30. Where were they going to take him?	to a _ _ _ _ _ _ _ _ _
4	Some friends wanted to take Harry to a concert. What kind of music?	_ _ _ _ _ _
5	What kind of party were his friends planning?	a _ _ _ _ _ _ _ _ party

Who:

6	What did Harry miss at 4 pm?	_ _ _ _ _ _
7	What was the name of the restaurant for the surprise?	_ _ _ _ _ ' _
8	Who was Harry's tennis partner?	_ _ _
9	Whose house was the surprise party in?	_ _ _ _ _ _ ' _

Post your solution to the puzzle by *(insert deadline)*.

---

5   Post the solution to the quiz above.

▶ Solution

Where: Harry caught the train to **Paris**.

Who: He went to meet his **twin** brother.

1	**P**resent		6	**T**ennis
2	**A**ppointment		7	**W**endy's
3	**R**estaurant		8	**I**an
4	**I**ndian		9	**N**atalie's
5	**S**urprise			

6   Post Task 4, which asks students to discuss the story of what actually happened that day. Set a deadline for posting ideas.

▶ Task 4: Interaction

Now discuss Harry's movements on that day. What do we know about where he went and what he did? Think about these questions:

What was the first thing we know he did? What time?

When did he get a phone call? Who was it from? Why was he excited?

Who did he phone? What time?

Why couldn't he phone anyone else?

When did he go to the bank? What did he get out of the bank and why?

Why did he catch a train to London? What time was the train?

Post your answers by *(insert deadline).*

---

7   When students have posted the events of Harry's morning, post the story.

▶ The story

Harry was adopted. He learned recently that he had a twin brother whom he had never met, because he had been adopted by a different family. He had been trying to contact this brother in order to meet him. On his birthday, Harry got up early and went to a breakfast meeting at work. He had arranged to have the rest of the day off, but agreed to go to the meeting. During the meeting, he got a phone call from his twin brother who lived in Paris. He was very excited and when his brother suggested that perhaps they could meet for lunch or dinner in Paris, he agreed. It was both their birthdays, after all! Harry remembered to cancel the dentist's appointment straight away, but was in a hurry to leave and catch a train to London and Paris, so thought he could phone and cancel other arrangements from the train. However, he left his phone behind by mistake, so could not contact anyone. He stopped briefly at the bank to change money for his trip and then caught the train to London in order to get the Eurostar train to Paris.

What do you think happened when the twins met to celebrate their birthdays? Post your ideas by *(insert deadline).*

---

8   Discuss students' ideas about the final question. Give any necessary language feedback and end the activity by thanking students for their participation.

▲ **Role cards for Disappearing act**

1 Sam: Harry's friend. You knocked on his door at 9 am to give him a present. He wasn't there. You left the present with a neighbour.

2 Mark: Harry's friend. You were due to meet him for a drink at 6 pm. You went to the café but he didn't turn up.

3 Ally: Dentist's receptionist. Harry phoned to cancel his appointment at about 9 am. It was hard to hear – a lot of people were talking.

4 Alex: Harry's friend. Three or four friends of Harry's were planning a surprise. You were going to take him to a restaurant for lunch. You planned to pick him up at his house at 12:30 pm.

5 Will: Harry's friend. You were going to have lunch with Harry at 1 o'clock but he didn't turn up.

6 Tom: Harry's cousin. Harry's father has been ill. He was in hospital in London and is now at home. He's not his real father, by the way: Harry was adopted.

7 Sally: You know that two friends of Harry's had bought him surprise tickets for an Indian music concert on the evening of his birthday.

8 Martha: Harry's friend. You know that some friends were organizing a surprise party for Harry on the evening of his birthday. They were going to pick him up from the tennis club at 5:30 pm and take him to Natalie's house for the party. You couldn't go, so you don't know if he went or not.

9 Tammy: Harry's friend. You had planned a surprise birthday lunch for Harry with three friends. You were going to pick him up at home at 12:30 pm and go to Wendy's restaurant. You arrived to pick him up, but he wasn't there. You went for lunch anyway!

10 Joe: Newsagent. You know Harry a little – he buys a paper at your shop. You saw him getting onto the London train at about 9:30 am.

11 Maria: Harry's friend. You bought him a ticket to come to an Indian music concert with you. You couldn't find Harry or contact him by phone so sold his ticket.

12 Sue: Harry's colleague. Harry was at the breakfast meeting at work. In the middle he got a phone call. He seemed very surprised and excited about the call. He made another call to his dentist and then left in a hurry. So much of a hurry that he left his mobile phone behind!

13 Ian: member of tennis club. You had a date to play a game of tennis with Harry at 4 pm. He never showed up.

14 Natalie: Harry's friend. You had planned a surprise party in the evening for Harry at your house. Friends were going to pick him up at the tennis club and bring him over for the party. But he wasn't at the tennis club! You couldn't reach him on the phone.

15 Neil: Bank manager. Harry came into the bank at about 9:15 am. He changed some money into euros.

16 Rob: Harry's friend. Harry told you he had just found out he had a twin brother he had never met. He was trying to contact him to arrange a meeting.

7   Feedback and assessment

This section looks at two areas in the forefront of online teaching, those of feedback and assessment. The increased use of new technologies in online education has led to many opportunities for new kinds of assessment, or provision of feedback. But they have also led to many challenges for the online instructor. It is perhaps beyond the scope of this book to cover these areas fully in depth, but they are nevertheless important enough to warrant some guidance here.

In this chapter we will talk about the importance of feedback and assessment in the kinds of activities we have proposed so far in the book. We will look in detail at how feedback can be given, and what kind of feedback options instructors have. We will also look at different options of what to assess in online interaction, and different examples of how this might be done.

Online feedback and assessment: opportunities and challenges

Assessment and feedback are increasingly forming a large part of the teacher's workload. The spread of online learning options for language courses has intensified this trend, and has required many to re-examine the use of technology in both areas. On the positive side, technology provides messages about learning, something that is arguably very helpful for learners. More and more programs and software make it possible to provide assessment with instant feedback. In addition, new learning platforms are beginning to move towards personalized feedback on tasks, based on algorithms which can track an individual learner's progress and even make recommendations on what to study or work on next. The potential use of such programs cannot be overestimated, as it is argued that they can take some of the burden off the teacher.

However, the areas of assessment and feedback on online interaction are different. Interaction across a discussion forum, or in a live chat, is not a product in the same way that a discrete exercise or composition is. Many language teachers are familiar with the student who scores very highly on a written placement test, but then can barely communicate when in class. While it may eventually be possible for a piece of software to recognize the accuracy, timeliness, relevance and quality of a student's contributions and interaction during a course, we feel that this is still some way off. It is also an area which is more subjective and, in our view, more requiring of a human touch.

Three purposes of feedback on interaction

Giving feedback on interaction can serve three purposes that are of importance to the language teacher:

- Firstly, feedback can act as encouragement to the learners to continue to interact, or to develop the interaction further and produce more language. A few words from the teacher in response to an early contribution in an online discussion or chat, for example, can help others to join in and give confidence to those who already have.

- Secondly, feedback can help improve accuracy during the interaction. Here, we imagine the kind of feedback that language teachers often give during speaking activities, when recasting or requesting clarification to make meaning clear.
- Thirdly, feedback can serve as language enrichment for future interaction. This can be in the form of vocabulary and grammatical enrichment, or functional enrichment when exploring how the same message can be conveyed in different ways.

Sometimes, feedback can serve more than one purpose at the same time. At times, it may even serve all three purposes. For this reason, it is a key tool in the online language teacher's kit.

Forms that feedback can take

As mentioned above, feedback can occur during or after an online activity. One form of feedback is encouragement, used to reward learners who have started interacting and to coax less willing participants to join in. This kind of feedback works best at the beginning and early stages of an online activity. Thanking and congratulating students at the end of an activity is also recommended.

Another kind of encouraging feedback is for the teacher to intervene in the interaction from time to time to respond to the content (and not the form) of what a student has written. This could be to express surprise, ask for clarification, or react in the same brief way that people react to each other's posts or comments on social media. On these occasions the teacher is almost formally joining the interaction activity, and there is a risk that students could begin to communicate more with the teacher than with each other. In these cases it is perhaps best to steer them back to interacting with each other and to take a back seat again.

Finally, feedback for language enrichment can also occur. This is perhaps more common at the end of an activity, but a feedback slot that includes guidance and correction on language can be used to reinvigorate an activity that has gone quiet. It may also provide an opportunity to widen or narrow the focus of the activity if interaction is drying up.

For any online activity that requires the students to interact by writing to each other, it would seem logical that the feedback is given in written form. However, the online medium allows for other forms of feedback as well, in several different media. Here are some examples:

- Create an audio recording in which you comment on different aspects of the interaction.
- Create a video recording in which you comment on different aspects of the interaction.
- Create a screencast in which you show the interaction that has taken place and, using a highlighting tool, focus on different aspects of what was written. To do this, you will need software for screencasting. There are a number of options available; you can find these online using the search term 'screencasting software' in a search engine. Russell Stannard has an excellent blog on this subject which relates to student individual writing, but could easily be used for other things (see http://russellstannard.com/).
- Create a more abstract visual kind of feedback. Using a word processor, you could copy and paste parts of an interaction task and make certain parts more visible and salient by using different colours and sizes, or you could make a word cloud containing the most common areas / errors / strong examples of language that occurred.

Feedback techniques

Aside from the form the feedback can take, there are different techniques that you can use to give feedback, in particular feedback for language enrichment. The following are six ways that feedback can be given at the end of an activity, either for explicit language correction or for extending the language that was produced.

Error correction 1
Collect a series of student-created sentences from the activity, some correct and others containing a language error. Mix these up and post them, asking students to identify which ones are correct and which are incorrect. At the end, ask students to suggest correct versions of the sentences.

Error correction 2
Similar to error correction 1, but here you select only examples of language produced that are incorrect. Ask students to try and correct the errors. To make sure everyone contributes, try gathering at least one error from each student. They then must locate their sentence and correct it.

Error correction 3
In this version, you explicitly highlight an error and give more detailed feedback on it. This is better for errors which are not as straightforward as spelling or grammar mistakes, and may just be unnatural or awkward-sounding language. Here is an example from an online discussion on school and work:

Thank you for all your contributions to the activity this week. I wanted to talk about some of the little mistakes that you made, but this time I will give you an explanation of the error. Many of these are examples of language that sounds a little bit unnatural but is otherwise correct! See below.

… at the entrance to mom's block.

All the vocabulary is fine here, but this sounds as if we all know the mother. Using the informal word *mom* and no possessive gives that impression. Also, *block* isn't clear on its own. This would be better: *… at the entrance to my mother's block of flats.*

… Since then, I spend the best time with my sweet nieces …

This is a grammar problem. With *since* we usually use a different tense. Yes! It should be the present perfect: *Since then, I've spent the best time …*

… I closed my time of being a coordinator …

No grammar error here, but the word choice of *close* isn't exactly right. It would sound better with the verb *finish*. The phrase is *finish + (time) + as*, or in this case: *I finished my time as a coordinator.*

Extending language 1

Identify a type of language that frequently occurred during the interaction, and suggest different ways that it can be expressed. Here is an example following a forum discussion on 'Superpowers':

The 'Superpowers' activity is now closed. Well done, everyone – there were some very creative suggestions! Here is some feedback on the language we produced here.

This activity used a lot of verbs for ability. Here are some different ways of expressing ability. Do you know if the verbs are followed by *-ing*, infinitive without *to*, or infinitive with *to*?

I can …

I am capable of …

My superpower allows me …

I'm able …

It enables me …

I have the ability …

I am competent at/in …

I am skilled at/in …

Post your answers below.

Extending language 2

Choose a piece of student writing from the interaction which is relatively correct, but perhaps too simple. Rewrite the piece, correcting the errors and making it a little more complex. Post the original and the rewritten one as an example, and ask students to identify what differences they can see.

Extending language 3

Here, you take examples of the language produced and suggest ways of making them more detailed. Provide some examples and ask students to go back and look at their original posts, then choose one to improve and post it again. Here is an example from a relatively short activity on food images:

Thanks, everyone, for your photos and participation in this short activity. There wasn't a lot of language for correction, because you all wrote in very good English! But, I thought we could use this activity to extend our vocabulary. For example: *I had peanut butter*. I could add more by saying *I had smooth, creamy peanut butter*.

Here are some adjectives we can use to describe food. The ones we use will depend on the food we are describing. You can check these in a dictionary if you don't know them.

sweet, sour, bitter, hot, raw, strong, stale, plain, fresh …

There are lots of ways of describing food with adjectives ending in *-y* (usually made from a noun or a verb + *y*), e.g. *spicy, chewy, creamy, greasy, juicy, meaty, smoky, tasty, watery, yummy …*

So, now try and describe your food again in the comments below. Add a suitable adjective or two (maximum two). I will then reply to your comment with feedback.

Assessment: what to assess

Informal and formal testing usually takes place at the beginning and end of most language courses, as well as at various points during a course itself. In terms of online assessment, some teachers may already have an automated online assessment tool; this could be in the form of a placement or diagnostic test, end-of-unit tests or end-of-course tests. These kinds of tests are usually based around discrete items of grammar or vocabulary, and to an extent reading and listening comprehension.

However, many of the activities in this book that focus on online interaction are based on a certain kind of writing skill: the skill of interacting with others online in a written form. In a sense, assessing this kind of language production is more similar to assessing speaking than it is to assessing formal writing (the kind of writing done for exam-type tasks, for example).

Assessing online discussions or chats has therefore always been an area of difficulty. As mentioned at the beginning of this chapter it is very hard, if indeed at all possible, for a piece of software or algorithm to do this in a satisfactory way, meaning that this element of a course needs to be assessed by another human being. The extra work involved in doing this might lead some to incline towards the kind of automated assessment mentioned before (i.e. grammar and vocabulary, basic listening and reading comprehension) but assessing online interaction can have three important benefits:

- It can give learners an indication of how they are doing in real-time produced language.
- It can encourage a higher quantity of student participation.
- It can encourage a higher quality of student participation.

So, if assessing online interaction is a part of your course, where do you begin? A logical starting point would be including the kind of criteria used in traditional writing assessments. Here are two such criteria:

- Accuracy: were the student's posts written clearly and in accurate language? Were there relatively few grammar and vocabulary mistakes? Bear in mind that 'accuracy' here is a relative term: the accuracy required for a real-time online chat may be different from that of other genres such as an essay or report. Accuracy here should therefore be seen through the prism of communicative effectiveness. Were the messages accurate enough to be understood by the reader?
- Range: were the student's posts written in language appropriate for his/her level? Did the student show attempts at expressing more complex ideas? Did the student 'play it safe' and use language too simple to really complete the task satisfactorily?

Assessing accuracy and range are two logical areas for the language teacher to start with, but because of the nature of online writing and interaction this may not be enough. Here is a list of other areas that could be included for assessment that are more pertinent to the kind of online interaction we have been promoting in this book:

- Promptness: did the student participate early enough in the activity to allow for interaction? Did the student respond promptly to questions asked by the teacher or others during the activity?
- Frequency: did the student participate actively, while not dominating the activity?
- Quality: was the content of the student's contributions complete and thoughtful, and did they offer new ideas or insights?
- Relevance: were the student's contributions relevant to the task? Did the student follow up on other people's points in a relevant manner?

- Interaction: did the student respond to others' contributions or simply post their own thoughts? Did the student engage in dialogue, or encourage the others to post? Did the student respond to questions or comments? Did the student observe 'netiquette', i.e. were posts courteous?

Any form of online assessment that aims to encourage positive washback in terms of interaction between participants should include at least some of the latter criteria.

Assessment: how to assess

For many teachers, a key purpose of assessment of discussion forums and chats is to ensure participation. A percentage of any grade or mark for assessment may be based purely on whether or not a student joined in the activity, regardless of the quality of his or her contributions. In some cases, the assessment may be based solely on participation. But it is worthwhile looking beyond this to incorporating some of the other criteria we mention above.

Once you have decided what criteria you are using for assessment, how do you do it? One way is to create rubrics, a tool long used in the evaluation of writing and speaking as a second language. A rubric defines the performance level for each activity element that is to be graded. Figure 7.1 shows rubrics for grammar and vocabulary control in an online writing activity used by the Universidad Peruana de Ciencias Aplicadas, Laureate International Universities, in Peru.

Criteria	1	2	3	4
Grammar	Sentence structure in the text shows a number of major grammar mistakes.	Sentence structure in the text shows a few major grammar mistakes.	Sentence structure in the text shows some minor grammar mistakes.	Sentence structure in the text shows no grammar mistakes.
Vocabulary	Text barely includes suitable vocabulary. Interference of Spanish is displayed. Mistakes affect comprehension.	Text includes somewhat moderate vocabulary. Some interference of Spanish is displayed.	Text includes moderate and adequate vocabulary. Little interference of Spanish is displayed.	Text includes very good use of vocabulary. No interference of Spanish is displayed.

Figure 7.1: Sample rubrics for grammar and vocabulary control

Figure 7.2 shows possible rubrics for promptness and frequency of posts, and interaction.

Criteria	1	2	3	4
Promptness and Frequency	Did not make the minimum required number of posts and/or posted late.	Made the minimum number of posts, did not post promptly or reply.	Made above the minimum number of posts, posted promptly and replied to posts promptly	Contributed frequently and posted early in the interaction; replied promptly to any questions
Interaction	Did not engage with any other contributions; did not refer to any other posts; made inappropriate contributions.	Engaged superficially with other contributions; did not encourage further interaction.	Engaged with other contributions and encouraged others to post; replied to posts and asked questions.	Engaged actively with other contributions; showed detailed reading of others' posts; asked and answered questions.

Figure 7.2: Assessment rubrics

If you are using rubrics, we recommend making them known to students as you assign the tasks, or at the beginning of the course if you are assessing interaction as a whole. Rubrics take time to create, but you could argue this is a good investment. When there are clear criteria at the beginning of a task, both student and teacher expectations are better addressed (Conrad and Donaldson, 2011, pp. 26–7).

A difficult choice for the online teacher is how to choose what exactly to assess in a series of online interaction tasks. Trying to assess all the contributions made by each student is a time-consuming process and, in cases where many contributions may have been very short, probably not worth the trouble. One possibility is to take a random sample of longer posts made by a student and base the assessment on those. Another variation would be to ask the student to select two or three of what they feel their best contributions were and submit those for assessment.

Peer and self-assessment

The value of peer assessment and self-assessment is increasingly being recognized. These two kinds of assessment contribute towards the longer term purpose of learning: 'helping learners become self-reliant, confident and able to make judgements about their own learning' (Nicol, 2010, quoted in JISC, 2010). Online peer assessment is not without its problems, partly because students will tend to be more generous to each other in terms of grades (Bouzidi and Jaillet, 2009).

Most peer assessment schemes also work with criteria and rubrics. If you are using or have developed these already, here are some tips on how to implement these in an online course:

- Provide an encouraging and supportive environment to reduce students' natural anxieties about peer evaluation; emphasize your rationale for using it and explain its benefits.
- Distribute examples of what you consider to be thoughtful, respectful, and constructive feedback.

- Develop clear evaluation criteria or rubrics and distribute them before students are required to submit an assignment, so students know how they will be evaluated.
- Consider allowing students to evaluate one another anonymously.

(Harriet W. Sheridan Center for Teaching and Learning)

The same method can be used for self-assessment, with students being given the criteria and then asked to evaluate their own writing against it. Another method would be to combine different kinds of assessment for an overall mark, e.g.:

- Participation: 10% of mark
- Teacher grade: 30% of mark
- Peer grade: 30% of mark
- Self-assessed: 30% of mark.

Finally, as mentioned above in *Assessment: how to assess*, students may make a selection of their own posts or activities to either self-assess or submit for peer assessment.

A final method of exploring self-assessment is to ask students to keep a regular journal during an online course. Not only can this serve as a tangible record of activities that they have carried out, a journal can also allow a space for students to reflect on their own learning process. If you introduce a journal element to a course, it is worth suggesting questions and prompts of what to write. Here are some examples:

Make a list of the activities we did this week and comment on which ones you liked and why.
Do you think you contributed to the activity? How well?
What was most difficult about the activities this week?
Do you feel you made a lot of errors in the activities? What kind of errors?

A final word on plagiarism

Plagiarism is the copying of others' ideas and words and using them as if they were your own without acknowledgement and citation. This issue often comes up while discussing online and distance work with learners, and we would like to close with a couple of words about it.

Many of the activities in this book which ask students to provide facts or arguments contain the instruction that students should do this in their own words and not simply cut and paste for online sources. However it is also worth making the general point at the start of a course that all work posted should be the student's original words, and that if others' ideas and words are used they should be acknowledged. Penalties for improper appropriation of others' ideas should be made clear; if you are assessing work formally you may like to disqualify work that contains plagiarism, or ask for it to be resubmitted. You will also need to teach the students an appropriate way of referencing and citing work that they use. Depending on the context in which you are working and the formality of the assessment system, this may involve an academic system such as Harvard, or a simpler, less formal system that you specify yourself, e.g. *X says that '… ' (URL).*

Students will need to know that you can detect plagiarism easily. Often the language or style of a cut and pasted extract will alert you to the fact that it is not the student's own work, but there are many plagiarism checkers available. There are many online services and tools for checking plagiarism, simply use the terms 'plagiarism checker' or 'plagiarism detector' in a search engine.

References

Bouzidi, L. and Jaillet, A. (2009) 'Can Online Peer Assessment be Trusted?', *Educational Technology and Society*, 12 (4), pp. 257–268.

Conrad, R. and Donaldson, A. (2011) *Engaging the Online Learner*, San Francisco: Wiley and Sons.

JISC (2010) *Effective Assessment in a Digital Age: A guide to technology-enhanced assessment and feedback*. Available online at: www.jisc.ac.uk/digiassess [Last accessed March 2016]

Nicol, D. (2010) 'From monologue to dialogue: Improving written feedback in mass higher education', *Assessment and Evaluation in Higher Education*, 35(5), pp. 501–517.

Russell Stannard's website. Available online at: http://russellstannard.com/ [Last accessed March 2016]

Harriet W. Sheridan Center for Teaching and Learning, Brown University. Available online at: www.brown.edu/about/administration/sheridan-center/teaching-learning/course-design/learning-technology/peer-assessment-online) [Last accessed March 2016]

Further reading

Attwell, G. (ed.) (2006) *Evaluating E-learning: A Guide to the Evaluation of E-learning,*

Evaluate Europe Handbook Series Volume 2. Available online at: http://pontydysgu.org/wp-content/uploads/2007/11/eva_europe_vol2_prefinal.pdf [Last accessed March 2016]

Hattie, J. (2012) *Visible Learning for Teachers*, Abingdon: Routledge.

Nicol, D.J. and Macfarlane-Dick, D. (2006) 'Formative assessment and self-regulated learning: A model and seven principles of good feedback practice', *Studies in Higher Education*, 31(2), pp. 199–218.

8 Task design

This chapter looks at different ways in which you can design your own tasks to generate online interaction. While the activities in this book have been designed for you to incorporate into your teaching practice easily, there may be times when you wish to create a task or series of tasks particular to your context or syllabus. Designing an online activity entails working through a sequence of choices, attempting in each case to make the choice that is most suitable for your students and which best fulfils the aims of what you want to practise. There is a checklist at the end of this chapter designed to guide you through this process.

In this chapter we will outline the choices to be made, with examples working through three example activities from start to finish, suggesting criteria for making each choice and ending with a framework of questions that you can use to guide your design process.

Choice 1: Topic or language practice?

The first and most obvious choice is whether you want an activity designed around a topic or around language practice, e.g. a lexical set, a grammatical structure or a set of functional exponents. This first choice and the one that follows may be dictated for you by the course you are following. Alternatively, you may be free to choose according to students' needs and wants.

Choice 2: Which topic? What language? What level?

You may choose a topic, e.g. sport; a lexical set, e.g. food; a grammatical pattern, e.g. present perfect; or a function, e.g. suggestions. Both the initial choice and the more specific choice of what language to be used within that choice will be governed by the level of the students you are teaching. Again, this second level of choices may be constrained by coursebook or syllabus, or you may be free to choose according to needs, wants, preferences and level of your students.

Choice 3: What activity type?

Now the choices begin to get more creative – but also more complicated! Before getting down to the fine detail of exactly how the activity will unfold and the precise sequence of tasks it will involve, allow yourself time to experiment and let your imagination wander! This is an enjoyable and exciting stage in the design process. We suggest using our five categories of activity types as a basis for this choice:
- **Personal:** do you want to give your students a more conversational task, based on sharing personal information, values and experiences?
- **Factual:** do you want to design a quiz, search or guessing game based on factual information?
- **Creative:** do you want your students to create a 'product' such as a story, advert, proverb or poem?
- **Critical:** do you want to give your students a discussion or debate task based on opinions and logical argument?

- **Fanciful:** do you want to give your students a task based on a fantasy situation where they have to use their imagination and perhaps role play?

There will be several possible choices available for any topic or language point. For example:
- Sport might lend itself to a critical discussion on sponsorship, a fanciful activity like inventing a sport, a factual sports quiz or a personal discussion on what sports people play.
- Food vocabulary could lend itself to an activity based on personal preferences, a factual guessing game or a more fanciful/creative activity where students design a menu for a special occasion or write adverts for food products.
- The present perfect could be practised via a creative pattern poem, where students write lines according to a prescribed pattern or formula (see Activity 4.4: *Colours*), via a factual information search with questions such as *How long have women been able to vote in New Zealand?* or via personal questions about life experiences. Or possibly a discussion on what experiences have been important in your life.

Of course, some activities may fall into two categories (e.g. students creating a story based on events from their own lives would be a combination of a personal and a creative activity).

Throughout this chapter, these three examples are used to illustrate how activities may be designed. It is important at this stage to let your mind roam free and come up with as many alternatives as possible. Try and brainstorm freely. Then take a step back and evaluate your ideas, asking yourself questions about which activity is likely to yield the best results.

This important choice will partly depend on:
- which activity type will suit your teaching point best and provide most practice. For example, personal questions, a pattern poem or a quiz can be designed to provide repeated use of the present perfect, whereas it would be hard to get such targeted use into a discussion, where students may well use the simple past instead.
- the level of your group. For example, for an elementary group, writing a menu for a café would be easier than writing a recipe or an advert.
- your class's preferences. They may, for example, enjoy creative activities but dislike discussions.
- what inspires you most! If you are enthusiastic about a new idea, then you are likely to put more energy into developing it and presenting it to the students in an engaging way.

Finally, be warned: there is the possibility that your choice of activity type at this point may not work as well as you thought when you come to the detail of ordering the steps in the activity. Always be prepared to go back and try something else!

Choice 4: Stimuli

All interaction tasks set up by the teacher involve some kind of stimulus to begin with. It is from this stimulus that the students will respond and then eventually interact. Here is a list of the different kinds of stimulus you could use:
- a picture
- a question or series of questions
- a sentence to complete

- a 'frame' or pattern for writing a poem
- a written text
- an audio or video text
- a provocative statement or statements
- a puzzle or a clue to a puzzle
- a challenge to the students to do something (e.g. post a picture).

Tasks can, of course, involve a combination of stimuli (e.g. a picture and a puzzle). The stimulus can come from the teacher, or can come from the students themselves.

The choice of stimulus will depend on three main factors:
- how engaging and likely to inspire student interest the stimulus is
- how much interaction it is likely to provoke
- the nature of the interaction it is likely to provoke.

✪ Working examples

A critical discussion on sport could begin with the teacher posting a provocative statement about corruption in sport; a fanciful menu-writing activity to practise food vocabulary could begin with the teacher posting an image of a café; a factual quiz about past events could begin with the teacher posting a question.

Choice 5: Interaction patterns

Once you have a stimulus, you then need to decide how the students are going to interact with it. This is where designing online activities begins to differ significantly from designing classroom activities. Interactive activities in the classroom involve all students speaking at once, interacting in pairs or groups or in a mingling activity. In online activities, there are two significant differences: students' contributions appear one at a time in a linear fashion, and everyone can see everything that is said. Even though private messages and sub-group chat rooms can create an information gap, many activities which will work in a classroom will not work online. For example, the popular mingling activity *Find someone who …* (where students have a list, e.g. *Find someone who likes cats / can play the guitar* etc., and have to walk around the classroom asking questions to find the people) will not work online because it will only be necessary to ask the questions once and then everyone can see the answers. The game would be over with a very short number of interactions, before everyone has had time to make a contribution. So care must be taken in designing activities that:
- actually involve students interacting with one another and not just posting individual responses
- produce a sufficient number of interactions of an appropriate length
- involve all students
- in the case of language practice activities, provide sufficient practice of the target language.

However, although there are different and greater constraints on designing online activities, online interaction can offer stimulating and challenging possibilities that are not so easily afforded in classroom interaction:

- Students have access to all the resources of the web. This means interaction can be designed to offer some autonomy. For example, instead of providing information, students can research it on their own and inform each other.
- Information gaps can be provided by the students themselves, e.g. a jigsaw reading activity, where students read different texts and then share information. In the classroom this involves texts given by the teacher, but in an online activity, students can look up different texts on a topic and then come together in the forum to share ideas.
- There is more possibility for students to play a greater part in stimulating and influencing the flow of activities, e.g. by posting their own pictures for comment.

Because of these design differences, online interaction patterns are different from classroom interaction patterns. Below are the six most common patterns used in this book, with examples.

Pattern 1: Open response

Group stimulus → individual response → interaction

This is the most common type of online task. The teacher posts a stimulus to the whole group and asks students to respond individually. The teacher may then respond to students' responses, or ask students to comment on what others wrote.

Example: see Activity 6.3: *Build a bio.*

Pattern 2: Guided response

Group stimulus → individual guided response

In this task type the teacher posts a stimulus to the whole group and then specifies the sort of response that is needed. This could be following a certain structure, using a certain set of words or some other kind of restriction. A third stage may follow where the students react to each other's responses.

Example: see Activity 2.5: *Don't you hate it when …?*

Pattern 3: Sequential stimulus

Group stimulus → individual response → stimulus → individual response

For this task type the teacher posts a stimulus to the whole group and students individually respond. Once all students have responded, the teacher posts another stimulus and students respond to that. This kind of stimulus–response–stimulus–response is most common in synchronous chats.

Example: see Activity 2.6: *Finish my sentence.*

Pattern 4: Chain reaction

Group stimulus → individual response/stimulus → individual response/stimulus

This kind of task could be described as a chain reaction. The teacher posts a stimulus. The first student responds, and this response is the new stimulus for the next student to respond. Collaboratively building a story, or activities in which the last post will dictate what the next post is are common types.

Example: see Activity 6.1: *Almost superpower.*

Pattern 5: Multiple stimuli

Individual stimulus → individual response → interaction

In this task type, the stimulus is different for each student. The teacher may choose a stimulus to assign each individual or get them to choose it themselves. The students then respond to the stimuli, and afterwards respond to other students' stimuli.

Example: see Activity 4.10: *Dream on*.

Pattern 6: Breakout room

Group stimulus → small group response → interaction

The teacher assigns the whole group a stimulus, but then puts students into pairs or small groups to formulate a response. Once this is done, the responses are shared with the whole class and the teacher invites students to interact based on this. An alternative could involve different stimuli for different groups at the beginning. This pattern will require the use of a tool which allows students to break away from the main chat area and work alone in groups (this feature is called a 'breakout room' in chat or webinar platforms).

Example: see Activity 4.5: *Design a festival*.

♻ *Working examples*

If we continue our three examples (the critical discussion on corruption in sport, the fanciful menu writing activity and the factual quiz practising the present perfect) we can see how selecting from these choices might work out in practice.

Sport

In the critical discussion, the teacher has posted a provocative statement as stimulus, e.g. *Sport is not fair or enjoyable any more: there is too much corruption*. The simplest way of getting responses to this would be to use Pattern 1: Open response and simply invite reactions to this statement. Then when all responses have come in, or as they are coming in, the teacher can invite students to comment on each other's opinions. Another, more structured way of opening up a discussion would be to use Pattern 2: Guided response. For example the teacher could assign students to Group A or Group B. Group A have to find examples that support the statement (e.g. in international competitions – look online for contemporary issues using the search term 'corruption in sport') while Group B find examples that contradict the statement (e.g. greater inclusion of disabled people). This could be further structured by using Pattern 6: Breakout room, where each group has preparation time within the group to discuss and find a list of examples to support their position. Then the groups come together and debate the proposition. Even more structure can be added in at this point, by giving students in each group a number and specifying an order for interaction, e.g. A1, B1, A2, B2. The students then have to produce argument and counter-argument as in a game of tennis.

A final stage could be built into any of these patterns, where students discuss what could be done about the problem of corruption.

The advantages of structuring the interaction patterns more tightly are:

- to give students more idea of what to contribute (Patterns 2 and 6)
- to give them more preparation time (Pattern 6)

- to ensure that everyone contributes (Pattern 6)
- to increase the number of interactions (Pattern 6 and the final stage option).

Menu writing

In the fanciful menu writing activity, the teacher has posted a picture of a café as stimulus. They could then use Pattern 1: Open response and ask students to write a menu for the café. This, however, only involves individual responses and there is no real incentive for students to read or interact with each other's menus. They could add a stage where students are asked to comment on each other's menus, saying what they would like to eat. In this case the teacher would need to build in a safeguard to ensure that everyone did not comment on the same menu, e.g. by including the instruction, *If someone has commented on a menu already, choose another menu.* Alternatively, they could choose Pattern 5: Multiple stimuli and ask students to find and post a picture of a restaurant and imagine what kind of menu the restaurant offers. Then they could ask students to choose a restaurant and order a meal, with the 'visiting' student acting as customer and the 'resident' student acting as waiter. Again, a control should be built in to ensure that everyone's restaurant is visited.

The advantages of this design are:
- The freedom for students to choose their own restaurant picture will result in more variety of menus (Italian, Chinese, etc.).
- This variety will give students more incentive to read the different menus.
- There is a real reason for choosing a restaurant.
- The dialogue between customer and waiter will result in more exchanges than if students simply commented on food they like (although, of course, this dialogue entails the students knowing 'restaurant' language like *Would you like to order?* as opposed to the simpler expressing likes/ dislikes language).

Quiz

In the factual present perfect activity, the teacher has chosen to post a question as stimulus: *How long have women had the vote in New Zealand?* This activity could be structured as interaction Pattern 3: Sequential stimulus. Students race to research and post the answer (they have been able to vote since 1893). Then the teacher posts the next quiz question, e.g. *How long has Madagascar been inhabited?* The requirement can be built in to comment on the fact that they have discovered, e.g. *New Zealand was the first country to give women the vote – I didn't know that!* Or *And all women didn't get the vote in Switzerland till 1971!* An alternative structure could be interaction Pattern 4: Chain reaction. In this pattern, the student who responds first poses the next question. However, it runs the risk that quicker students will get more practice and some students may be left out, so an additional constraint should be built in, for example, specifying an order for the chain reaction by giving each student a number. Alternatively, Pattern 4 could be preceded by a breakout room activity as in the sport discussion, where students have time to prepare their quiz questions in advance.

The advantages of the different patterns are:

- Pattern 3, with the requirement to comment, has the advantage of encouraging more engagement with and response to the facts. However, it provides less focused practice of the target language, since comments may well not include the present perfect.
- Pattern 4, with the order of questions specified, has the advantage of providing practice in question forms as well as affirmatives. It could also be structured to involve *Yes/No* questions (e.g. *Have people lived in Madagascar since prehistoric times?*) and negatives (e.g. *No, they haven't. People have only lived there for about 2,000 years.*).

Pattern 4, preceded by a breakout room in two teams, gives more preparation time for questions and increases the number of interactions.

It can be seen from the above examples that there is considerable flexibility in choosing interaction patterns, but that, depending on the activity and aim, some may be preferable to others.

Choice 6: Synchronous or asynchronous?

All of these interaction patterns can be used synchronously or asynchronously. You do not necessarily need a special platform like a chat room or webinar for synchronous communication: you can set up synchronous communication on a social media platform by specifying that everyone should join the group at a certain time. Your choice here may well be dictated by your circumstances. For example, if you are teaching in a blended learning situation and set online tasks for homework, you may want to give a longer time period for posting, rather than asking students to be available for a specified time. If you are teaching an online course, you may have to take account of different time zones, and asynchronous interaction may be your best choice.

Having said this, some interactions and activities may lend themselves better to one format than the other. In general, quick-fire activities and chain reactions where students have to post single sentences in response to a stimulus and then perhaps set the next stimulus for reaction, may be more dynamic in synchronous format, whereas activities that require reflection and thought, and longer responses, like some critical or creative activities, may work better in an asynchronous format.

✪ Working examples
In our three examples, the present perfect quiz is a chain reaction which might work better in a synchronous environment.

Choice 7: Staging and instructions

Once you have been through all five choices, you will need to consider carefully the exact staging of the activity and write clear instructions for the students for each stage. It is important to break the activity up into separate tasks and give instructions for each in a separate post, rather than giving all the instructions for the whole activity at once. It is also important to set a deadline for completion of each separate task. In these two ways instructions for and staging of online activities differ significantly from a classroom activity, where a worksheet with several stages or questions may be given to students to work through at their own pace.

❦ **Working examples**

Sport

In our first example activity, the critical discussion on sport, the stages and instructions could look like this using Pattern 6:

- Stage 1: Teacher divides students into two teams and assigns each team a chat room or private message group.
- Stage 2: Teacher posts a provocative statement together with instruction to each team and sets a deadline.
- Stage 3: Teacher gives students in each group a number and posts instruction for the two teams to come together and post their arguments one at a time in the specified order.
- Stage 4: Teacher asks students a new question.
- There could be an optional extra Stage 5 where students are asked to use ideas from the argument to write an essay as a follow-up activity.

The posts with instructions could look like this:

1 Stage 1: Private message students.

> For this activity you will work in two teams. Ana, Paolo, Katerina and Tomoko: you are Team A. Soly, Xuen, Beatrix and Mateo: you are Team B. I have set up private messages / chat rooms for each team. Can you first of all check that you can find your team's chat room and say Hi to each other?

2 Stage 2: Set up a forum and give it a name (this is usually the name of the activity). Post Task 1 and set a deadline for completing the task.

> **Task 1**
>
> Here is a statement about sport today:
>
> *Sport is not fair or enjoyable any more: there is too much corruption.*
>
> Team A: Work together to support this statement. Find as many examples of corruption in sport as you can. Share your examples and make a list.
>
> Team B: Work together to contradict this statement. Find as many positive examples of sport doing good and being enjoyable as you can. Share your examples and make a list.
>
> Complete this research task by *(insert deadline)*.

3 Stage 3: Go through Task 1. Then post Task 2 and set a deadline for completing the task.

> **Task 2**
>
> Well done, everyone – you have found a number of good examples! Now you are going to argue!
> I'm going to give each of you a number.
> Team A: Ana A1, Paolo A2, Katerina A3, Tomoko A4.
> Team B: Soly B1, Xuen B2, Beatrix B3, Mateo B4.
> You will post in this order: A1, B1, A2, B2, A3, B3, A4, B4.

> Come together in the main forum now.
>
> Ana (A1): begin by choosing one example from your list in support of the statement and posting your argument, e.g.:
>
> *There is so much corruption in sport nowadays that games are no longer fair or enjoyable. For example, last week a referee was found guilty of match fixing.*
>
> Soly (B1): reply using one of your examples, beginning *Yes, but …*, e.g.:
>
> *Yes, but disabled people have more equal opportunities to take part in sports than they did and that makes sport fairer for everyone.*
>
> Then it is Paolo's (A2) turn, and so on.
>
> You have until *(insert deadline)* to complete posting. Enjoy the discussion!

4   Stage 4: Post Task 3, responding to Task 2, and set a deadline for completing the task.

> **Task 3**
>
> That was a great discussion! Now I'd like you to think of solutions to the problem of corruption in sport. How can we fight it or eliminate it? Post your suggestions by *(insert deadline)*.

5   Stage 5 (optional follow-up): Post Task 4, responding to Task 3, and set a deadline for completing the task.

> **Task 4**
>
> Some great suggestions there!
>
> Your final task is to write a short essay. Look back over the discussion and organize the arguments for and against the statement and the solutions into three paragraphs:
>
> *Sport is a global symbol of fair play and provides enjoyment for many people …*
>
> *However, it is also a multi-million dollar industry and corruption is a real problem …*
>
> *It is important to fight against corruption in sport …*
>
> Send me your essays by *(insert deadline)*.

Some points to note about the staging and instructions:
- Stage 1 (first post) makes sure that students can access the chat room / breakout / private message facility. This is important if you are doing a complex activity with groups and prevents later breakdown of the activity.
- Stage 2 (second post with Task 1) sets a deadline for posting. All tasks should have a deadline for completing the task and posting results. It is important not to let the activity drag.
- Stage 3 (third post with Task 2) nominates students and gives them a number to let them know exactly what they have to do. It also gives concrete examples. This is important to give students an idea of the kind of contribution they need to make.

- Stage 4 (fourth post with Task 3) is a looser task than the previous posts. This takes account of the fact that they have put in a considerable amount of preparation already and will be prepared to interact in a freer format.
- Stage 5 (fifth post with Task 4) gets them to use their ideas as basis for an argumentative essay and structures this into topic paragraphs.

Menu writing

In the fanciful menu-writing activity, the stages and instructions could look like this using Pattern 5:

- Stage 1: Teacher posts a picture of a café with a menu and asks students what they would like to order for the menu.
- Stage 2: Teacher asks students to post a picture of a restaurant with a menu.
- Stage 3: Teacher asks students to 'visit' a restaurant they like and order a meal.

The posts with instructions could look like this:

1   Stage 1: Post Task 1 and set a deadline for completing the task.

Task 1

Here is a picture of a restaurant with the restaurant menu.

What would you like to eat?

Post your answer by *(insert deadline)*.

---

2   Stage 2: Post Task 2 and set a deadline for completing the task.

Task 2

Now you!

Find a picture of a restaurant.

Imagine … what is the restaurant menu?

Post your picture and your menu by *(insert deadline)*.

---

3   Stage 3: Post Task 3 and set a deadline for completing the task.

Task 3

What great menus … I feel hungry!

Now choose a restaurant. Imagine you are a customer. Your partner will be the waiter.

Here is some useful language to start with:

Waiter: *Can I help you?*

Customer: *Good evening. I'd like a table for two.*

Waiter: *There's one over here. Here's the menu.*

Customer: *Thank you.*

> Waiter: *Are you ready to order?*
>
> Customer: *Yes, I'd like …*
>
> Rule: If there is one customer already at a restaurant, then it is 'full'! Choose another restaurant!
>
> Finish your 'meal' by *(insert deadline)*.

Some points to note about the staging and instructions:

- In comparison to the previous activity, the language in the instructions is much simpler and reflects the level that this activity is designed for.
- The activity is also much simpler conceptually, with fewer, simpler stages. This is important for lower-level students.
- Note the importance of modelling at this level. The teacher's first post (Task 1) is a model of what the students will have to do in the next stage (Task 2). The third post (Task 3) also includes a sample beginning of the role play. This will give students a clear idea of what is required and also help them to get started.
- The third post (Task 3) also includes a safeguard 'rule' to prevent the possibility that many students might choose the same restaurant, leaving other students with no interaction.

Quiz

In the factual present perfect quiz activity, the stages and instructions using Pattern 4 could look like this:

- Stage 1: Teacher posts the first question introducing the rules for the game.
- Stage 2: Teacher posts allocating a number for each student with the rules for the chain reaction.
- Stage 3: Teacher invites students to comment on surprising facts.

The posts with instructions could look like this:

1 Stage 1: Post Task 1 and set a deadline for completing the task.

> **Task 1**
>
> Today we're going to play a game. I'm going to post a question. The first person to answer correctly gets a point. The question is:
>
> *How long have women had the vote in New Zealand?*
>
> Please reply using *for…* or *since …* , e.g. *for 200 years / since 1815.*
>
> Post your replies by *(insert deadline)*.

2 Stage 2: Post Task 2 and set a deadline for completing the task.

Task 2

Soly, you get 1 point! Well done!

Now, I will give you all a number: Ana 1, Paolo 2, Katerina 3, Tomoko 4, Soly 5, Xuen 6, Beatrix 7, Mateo 8.

Now, please make up your own questions and post in this order.

Ana: please begin. Make a question about a historical fact. The rules are:

You use the present perfect with *how long, for and since.*

You can use a *How long* question, e.g. *How long have people lived in Madagascar?*

Or you can use a *Yes/No* question, e.g. *Have people lived in Madagascar since prehistoric times? Have people lived in Madagascar for over a million years?*

Try to be the first to answer. Remember the first answer may not be correct – so everyone should post!

When everyone has posted, then it is Paolo's (number 2) turn to post a question.

You have until *(insert deadline)* to post questions and answers.

---

3   Stage 3: Post Task 3 and set a deadline for completing the task.

Task 3

Well done, everyone! Tomoko was the winner with 4 points – but everyone else was very close!

Now look back at the historical facts. Does anything surprise you? Choose one fact that surprises you and comment, e.g.:

New Zealand was the first country to give women the vote – I didn't know that!

And all women didn't get the vote in Switzerland till 1971!

Post your comments by *(insert deadline)*.

Some points to note about the staging and instructions:
- Again, examples of how to contribute are given. These are quite precisely specified to direct students into using the target language (instead of perhaps posing questions like *When did women in New Zealand get the vote?*).
- Stage 3 again allows students to comment and give personal reactions in a freer format without necessarily using the target language. This is because some of the facts posted elicit surprise and personal reaction, but the tight format of the competition has not allowed for comment up till then.

To sum up, here are some criteria for dividing the activity into tasks and writing instructions:
- Activities need to be clearly broken down into small tasks.
- It is important to check students' understanding of how to interact in a complex task.
- Tasks should be conceptually appropriate for level: lower levels need simpler tasks.
- A deadline needs to be set in every task for posting.
- Clarity of instructions is vital. Instructions should be written in short sentences – one stage, one sentence – and language adapted for level.
- It is very important to give examples of what contributions are required from students.

- Particularly at lower levels, the first post by the teacher should provide a model of what to do.
- It is important to build in rules and safeguards to ensure even interaction.
- Positive feedback on a previous stage is a good way of introducing instructions for the next stage.

A checklist of questions for task design

This checklist is a summary of the criteria explained above at each stage of the design process. Here, it functions as a concise list of questions to guide you through the process of designing your own activities.

Choice 1: Topic or language practice?
- What kind of activity do you want/need to design? Do you want/need an activity designed around a topic or around language practice – a lexical set, a grammatical structure or functional language?
- What would be most useful for your students at this point in the course?

Choice 2: Which topic? What language? What level?
- What level are your students? Is the class homogenous or mixed ability?
- What have they just learned (what topic/language) and what practice could benefit them?
- What do you think they would like best and what do you think they need most? Can you balance these wants and needs?

Choice 3: What activity type?
- Personal: do you want to give your students a more conversational task, based on sharing personal information, values and experiences?
- Factual: do you want to design a quiz, search or guessing game based on factual information?
- Creative: do you want your students to create a 'product' like a story, advert, proverb or poem?
- Critical: do you want to give your students a discussion or debate task based on opinions and logical argument?
- Fanciful: do you want to give your students a task based on a fantasy situation where they have to use their imagination and perhaps role play?
- What do you think they would like best and will engage them, and what do you think they need most? Can you balance these wants and needs?

Choice 4: Stimuli
- What stimulus will you use to initiate interaction?
  - a picture
  - a question or series of questions
  - a sentence to complete
  - a 'frame' or pattern for writing a poem
  - a written text
  - an audio or video text
  - a provocative statement or statements
  - a puzzle or a clue to a puzzle
  - a challenge to the students to do something (e.g. post a picture)

- How engaging and likely to inspire student interest is the stimulus you have chosen?
- How much interaction is it likely to provoke?
- What kind of interaction is it likely to provoke?

Choice 5: Interaction patterns
- What interaction pattern suits your activity best?
  - Pattern 1: Open response
  - Pattern 2: Guided response
  - Pattern 3: Sequential stimulus
  - Pattern 4: Chain reaction
  - Pattern 5: Multiple stimuli
  - Pattern 6: Breakout room
- Is this pattern likely to engage students and make them want to contribute?
- Does this pattern actually involve interaction and not just individual responses?
- Does this pattern produce a sufficient number of interactions?
- Does this pattern involve all students?
- In the case of language practice activities, does this pattern provide sufficient practice of the target language?

Choice 6: Synchronous or asynchronous?
- Is the activity best carried out synchronously in a chat room or webinar, or asynchronously in a forum, with appropriate deadlines for the different tasks?

Choice 7: Staging and instructions
- Is your activity clearly broken down into small tasks?
- Have you checked students' understanding of how to interact, especially in a complex task?
- Are the tasks conceptually appropriate for level: lower levels, simpler tasks?
- Have you set a deadline for posting?
- Are your instructions clear and simple? Instructions should be written in short sentences: one stage, one sentence.
- Have you given examples of what contributions are required from students?
- Do your posts provide a model of what to do, particularly important at lower levels?
- Have you built in rules and safeguards to ensure even interaction?
- Can you include positive feedback on a previous stage before introducing instructions for the next stage?

Index

Names of activities are in **bold**, locators for figures and tables are in *italics*.

e-Source

SYSTEM REQUIREMENTS

Operating system and browsers
e-Source runs on most operating systems and browsers, including Internet Explorer 8 and above, Mozilla Firefox, Google Chrome, and Safari.

Hardware
You won't need any other hardware to run e-Source other than your computer. However, to listen to audio resources, you may need external speakers.

Internet connection
e-Source performs best over a broadband internet connection.

Additional software
To play flash content, a flash player [http://get.adobe.com/flashplayer/] will need to be installed.

TERMS AND CONDITIONS OF USE

Full terms and conditions of use are available at:
http://esource.cambridge.org/Terms-of-Use.pdf

CPSIA information can be obtained
at www.ICGtesting.com
Printed in the USA
LVHW101215260319
611869LV00004B/8/P